The Fake News Panic of a Century Ago

The Fake News Panic of a Century Ago

The Discovery of Propaganda and the Coercion of Consent

Second Edition

For Jane—
With many thanks—
and all best wishes!!
Lee Huebner

Lee W. Huebner

cognella®

SAN DIEGO

Bassim Hamadeh, CEO and Publisher
Carrie Baarns, Manager, Revisions and Author Care
Kaela Martin, Project Editor
Celeste Paed, Associate Production Editor
Emely Villavicencio, Senior Graphic Designer
Alexa Lucido, Licensing Manager
Natalie Piccotti, Director of Marketing
Kassie Graves, Senior Vice President of Editorial
Jamie Giganti, Director of Academic Publishing

cognella® | ACADEMIC PUBLISHING
3970 Sorrento Valley Blvd., Ste. 500, San Diego, CA 92121

Contents

Preface

M ark Twain is said to have said, "History doesn't repeat itself, but it often rhymes." If this is the case, then one might go on to say that there are moments when the resonance between two historical moments is so strong that it compels our continuing attention. Perhaps we can learn something from the past, we hope, that can help us cope with the present and, just maybe, help us shape the future.

This book began as an exploration into the history of ideas, with a focus on ideas that were much in the air as a hopeful new twentieth century moved from its first to its third decade. Publicity was one such topic, spurred by the potentials of new mass communication technologies. Meanwhile, the concepts of human suggestibility and social instability also became the focus of widespread anxiety. As the years progressed, many people in the United States and elsewhere became increasingly concerned that these processes could threaten the viability of democracy itself. A relatively new term that reflected these challenges came into popular usage, the concept of propaganda.

What became increasingly clear as these discussions proceeded, of course, was that none of these realities was particularly new. The idea that new communications techniques could alter personal and social behavior was at least as old as ancient Greece. Socrates, after all, fretted about the impact of a new technology called "writing." Plato warned that democracy would inevitably lead to tyranny. Aristotle worried that democracies would not thrive outside of intimate, local environments. The printing press 500 years ago brought enlightenment to some but widespread chaos and conflict as well, "fostering manias and panics … millenarian sects and witches' crazes," as the historian Niall Ferguson recently reminded us. Similarly, hopes for the telegraph, radio, television, and the internet were quickly matched and often overtaken by evidence of their unavoidable dangers and disappointments.

Such historical "rhymes" abound, of course, but the purpose of this study is to explore the ways in which a combination of variables a century ago joined to produce a moment in American history that echoes our present moment in remarkable ways. In both eras what began as a new sense of media potential turned into skepticism about media reliability and eventually into cynicism about media manipulation.

Susanne Langer is quoted in the pages that follow as suggesting that we sometimes see only those things that we have names for. The name that seems to enter almost every conversation about the shape of media today is *fake news*. A century ago, the word was *propaganda*. The two words have been used, then and now, in very similar ways, usually to discredit unwelcome information. And in both cases it is not too much to say that what started out as a curiosity evolved over time into a neurosis and, eventually, in many cases, into an obsession.

Both *fake news* and *propaganda* are terms that were used to describe deliberate efforts to sway public opinion by inventing false stories—atrocity stories, for example, about the warring powers in the early days of the First World War. Before the war, however, the term *propaganda* was often used, sometimes interchangeably, with the word *publicity*, and its most familiar application was in describing the foreign mission arm of the Roman Catholic Church, the College of Propaganda. Over time, however, the propaganda terminology took on a decidedly pejorative connotation. It was commonly applied to a wide range of public messages: political and governmental rhetoric, ideological and religious advocacy, news stories, educational campaigns, and business and commercial persuasion. More than that, in both centuries, propaganda discussions were not limited to describing or discrediting particular persuasive efforts. What the obsession often meant was a growing public unreadiness to believe *any* story—ushering in the specter, then and now, of a postfact, posttruth world.

This book begins by describing two major developments that contributed to the "discovery" of propaganda a century ago. The first was a shift in the landscape of human psychology, an intensifying realization that that the public is a less rational entity than many had liked to claim, and that appeals to emotions, fears, desires, and resentments could short-circuit the reasoning mind. The second development was a process of social upheaval described by some as a delocalization of daily life, a distension of social arrangements, and, indeed, a globalization of human connection as significant as the transformation that has more recently gone by that name. In both cases, the psychological and social commentaries of a century ago can readily—and usefully—be read as insightful descriptions of what has been happening in our contemporary world.

This volume goes on to follow six well-known leaders in early twentieth century America who took these developments very seriously and who wrestled seriously with their implications. Two (Ivy Lee and Edward Bernays) were principle founders of the new profession of public relations. Two (George Creel and Woodrow Wilson) forged what was then the biggest war propaganda machine in human history. Two others (John Dewey and Walter Lippmann) were among the leading political philosophers of the epoch. All six were prolific speakers and writers. All six had long and influential careers. They wrote a lot, they revised a lot, they thought a lot, and in some cases they even recanted—at least a bit—as they tried in very different ways to come to terms with the intellectual, political, and commercial consequences of a new communications era.

The central problem for all of them was to reconcile the need for public cohesion with the ideal of public consent. To foster social order had once seemed largely a matter of coercion—power went to those who could, in the end, command the greatest physical, economic, or religious power. The progressive hope through the ages was that power might increasingly go to those who could foster the greatest public consent. To do that had often been seen as a matter of leadership, of persuasive skill, of argumentative prowess, of rhetorical accomplishment. But the growing question, especially in a changing media environment, was and still is just where leadership and persuasion, argument and advocacy end and where embellishment, spin, propaganda, and demagoguery begin.

What became dramatically apparent to many in the early years of the previous century was that public language—the great instrument for generating public consensus—could itself be weaponized, and on a far-reaching scale. That realization created an intellectual crisis for many. Is the notion of democracy then itself outdated—or at least in need of new definitions? What happens to the consent of the governed when the governed can so readily be confused, distracted, or simply misled? What happens to the consent of the governed when consent itself can be coerced? These are among the questions that will recur throughout this volume.

It should be mentioned that this second edition is a much-rewritten version of a first edition, which was also titled *The Fake News Panic of a Century Ago.* Its subtitle then was *Reflections on Globalization, Democracy, and the Media,* and a number of reflective essays in that volume—best summarized by the subtitle of the earlier edition—do not appear in this edition. The purpose of this new edition is to focus most sharply on the propaganda phenomenon of the early twentieth century, why it emerged when it did, what its consequences were, and how it might inform our thinking about our own current challenges.

This discussion owes a great deal to a variety of books, articles, lectures, interviews, and conversations in which this writer has been fortunate enough to share over many years of professional activity in the worlds of international media and education. Many, but surely not all, are mentioned in the source notes at the end of this volume. A remarkable array of students, mentors, colleagues, friends, and family members have also been a central part of this research and reflection process, and their contributions are also most gratefully acknowledged.

CHAPTER 1

Old Realities and New Perceptions

The twentieth century began, it might be figuratively be said, on Wednesday, June 8, 1898, as Theodore Roosevelt stood at dockside in Tampa, Florida, loading his company of Rough Riders aboard ships that would take them to help win the Spanish-American War on the battlefields of Cuba.

But there were too many soldiers and too few ships. Some men and horses would have to be left behind.

Roosevelt noticed two civilians standing nearby watching over a huge tripod and camera. When he asked who they were, the men reportedly responded, "We are the Vitagraph Company, Colonel Roosevelt, and are going to Cuba to take moving pictures of the war."

"The photographers found themselves being escorted up the gang-plank," according to Roosevelt biographer Edmund Morris, identifying Roosevelt as already "America's greatest master of press relations" and quoting him as saying, "I can't take care of a regiment but I might be able to handle two more."

Roosevelt was already something of a celebrity, especially in New York after brief stints as a state assemblyman, a US civil service commissioner, and a New York City police commissioner. He had resigned as assistant secretary of the US Navy after war was declared in 1898. Within a month, he was leading his troops on horseback and then on foot in a bloody and much-heralded charge up San Juan Hill (or, at least, a nearby promontory).

Roosevelt's popularity skyrocketed. By the end of the year, he had been elected governor of New York State. Two years later he was vice president, and a year after that, following President McKinley's assassination, Roosevelt succeeded him as president of the United States.

The dockside scene in Tampa was a symbolic moment in many ways. It was a telling juncture in the development of mass media; Vitagraph was a leader in developing the newsreel, and Roosevelt's warm welcome aboard for the photographers reflected his enthusiasm for the growing role of publicity in politics. But that's not all. At least some of the footage that later appeared on American screens seems to have been staged not in Cuba but in the hills of New Jersey. That was not

Roosevelt's doing, but it nonetheless illustrated early on the potential uses of "fake news." Or at least, "fake newsreels."

One other major change in American life is symbolized by the dockside story. Roosevelt's was the largest armed force, up to that moment, that had ever left American shores, about to take on a major European state. The war would establish the United States as a significant player in world affairs, with overseas territorial possessions (like the Philippines and Puerto Rico) and with such diplomatic clout that Roosevelt would win the Nobel Peace Prize in 1905 for negotiating a settlement to the Russo-Japanese War. His pet project, the development of the Panama Canal, became a prominent symbol of an increasingly globalized world. Thomas Friedman, even as he became a prominent analyst of a great new global age a century later, described the Roosevelt period as the "first great era" of globalization. In fact, he said, "It turns out that the roughly 75-year period from the start of World War I to the end of the Cold War was just a long time-out between one era of globalization and another."

***

Domestic changes were also dramatic. The economist Robert J. Gordon, in his 2016 study, *The Rise and Fall of American Growth*, contends that even the recent digital revolution has not transformed the spectrum of daily life as much as did a host of new technologies just before and after 1900. He mentions electric lighting (indoors and out), indoor plumbing, vast new railroad networks, streetcars, automobiles, the popularization of telegraph and telephone messaging, the cheap production of mass circulation newspapers and centrally produced magazines (and sales catalogs!), and then the early stages of motion pictures and even radio.

As media voices multiplied, the competition for audience attention often put a premium on more extreme and sensationalized content, witness the rise of "yellow journalism" at the end of the nineteenth century. Such impulses played a role in the onset of the Spanish-American War, including the unproven but much-headlined charge that Spanish weapons had blown up the US battleship Maine. Indeed, a very early use of the term "fake news" has even been traced to this period.

Many were quite bewildered by all of these new challenges. Their reactions strikingly resemble those of the present day. As one goes back to read their words, one can easily imagine that one is reading quite recent blogs, opinion columns, and interpretive articles.

Another Northwestern University professor, Robert Wiebe, in his widely cited 1967 study, *The Search for Order*, described the situation this way:

> The precipitant of the crisis was a widespread loss of confidence in the powers of the community, [as] countless citizens in towns and cities across the land sensed that something fundamental was happening to their lives, something they had not willed and did not want, and they responded by striking out at whatever enemies their view of the

word allowed them to see. They fought, in other words, to give their lives meaning. But it had already slipped beyond their grasp.

Among the targets identified by the restless populist impulses of the day were the great corporations of the country, the all-powerful monopolies, and their financial partners on Wall Street and in distant foreign capitals. Then as now, global conspiracy theories abounded.

At the same time came the effective disappearance of America's opportunity-enhancing western frontier, even as the American population itself seemed to be changing rapidly. What many saw, in Wiebe's words, was that

> the true and simple America [was] in jeopardy from foes of extraordinary, raw strength, huge, devouring monopolies, swarms of sexually potent immigrants, and the like. ... Mixing contempt with fear, natives pictured the newcomers as dispirited breeders of poverty, crime, and political corruption, and simultaneously as peculiarly powerful and subversive whose foreign ideologies were undermining American society.

Roman Catholics were often singled out for hostile comment, reflecting age-old religious and cultural animosities that parallel the animus directed against Muslims in a later era. What was unfamiliar was suspicious; what came from far away was particularly suspect. Wiebe added this striking comment to his discussion: "Nor did the term 'alien' necessarily mean foreign in a strict sense." Major cities at home and abroad were increasingly described as elitist dens of iniquity, harboring those who were indifferent and antagonistic to the fate of traditional American communities.

As these feelings of popular dislocation surged, a convenient target of complaint was the new power of communications media. This pattern of media-demonization would grow as the new century crept on. By the late 1920s the perceptive American philosopher John Dewey would sum things up in these words:

> We live exposed to the greatest flood of mass suggestion that any people has ever experienced. The need for united action, and the supposed need of integrated opinion and sentiment, are met by organized propaganda and advertising. The publicity agent is perhaps the most significant symbol of our present social life. There are individuals who resist; but, for a time at least, sentiment can be manufactured by mass methods for almost any person or any cause.

Susanne Langer has written that we only see that which we have names for. Such was the case with the newly popular word *propaganda*. People defined it in a variety of ways, agreeing generally that it applied, for better or worse, to purposeful communication in the public forum, or as Harold Lasswell later wrote, "acts of advocacy in mass communications." But most of the massive new commentary about propaganda, then and since, has seen the term as a distinctly pejorative one. Walter Lippmann would suggest a pithy definition in a 1927 lecture, "The art of controlling judgment by providing false images to awaken prejudice."

It was not that people had only just learned to propagandize. People had been lying to one another since the beginning of human history. The Ten Commandments warn against "bearing false witness," and one can infer that there was a fair amount of false witnessing going on in Old Testament times. Many leaders from ancient times to the present day have found it useful to replace facts with myths. One dramatic case was the Donation of Constantine, a document forged in the eighth century that claimed that the Roman emperor back in the fourth century had donated authority over Rome and western parts of the Roman Empire to the Pope. The document was used to support major church claims to secular and financial power throughout the Middle Ages. The church itself detected and exposed the forgery in the fifteenth century, but for some eight centuries it had helped shape much of Western history.

Nor is that story at all atypical. A steady stream of political, scientific, entertainment, and journalistic scams have seized and often preoccupied public attention over time, many with long-lasting consequences. Consider, for example, the counterfeit science of eugenics and its pervasive racist influence, or the anti-Semitic impact of the forged Protocols of the Elders of Zion through much of the twentieth century.

What was new in the early twentieth century, then, was not the existence of propaganda but rather the public awareness of its potential power. And that awareness turned steadily into an obsession, especially as people realized that there was now a new word for it.

The word *propaganda* itself had its own independent and often respectable history before it took on its new significance. The Roman Catholic Church began to use the Latin word in the seventeenth century to denote its mission activities—designed, of course, to counter the impact of the Protestant Reformation by propagating the faith, much as ancient Roman farmers had propagated their crops. An investigation of old dictionaries points to several secular uses of the term in the early nineteenth century, with a pejorative connotation creeping in by the 1850s, often linked to the messages of secret societies.

The word's growing popularity in the first part of the twentieth century was also spurred by its novelty. Propaganda was a strange-sounding word and fun to repeat. At first, in fact, it was used rather proudly by the proponents of constructive publicity. It helped them dramatize their own media initiatives. But it quickly took on grim connotations. And the major reason was not so much the boasts of purposeful advocates but rather the word's utility as a way to discredit opponents. You didn't like what someone was saying? Well, of course, it was just "propaganda." It was "fake news."

What the "discovery" of propaganda implied for many was a serious threat to the very concept of democratic government, challenging the idea that leaders could organize public consent without coercing it.

For much of human history, the power to coordinate social activity largely depended on the amount of coercive force a prospective leader could bring to the task. The promise of democracy was that leaders and ideas could compete for approval through exchanges of words rather than physical encounters. But what if the words themselves turned out to be weapons? What if verbal communication could be used consistently in ways that circumvented rational functions? How would people grapple with the challenges of self-governance if misinformation or disinformation could be systematically used to confuse or mislead the public? In that case all democratic bets might be off.

What the discovery of propaganda implied, in short, was that persuasion, the great democratic method for reconciling leadership and consent, was now suddenly itself seen as a fearful instrument of coercion.

***

As the word *propaganda* was popularized, it became a convenient way to diagnose what had gone awry with American democracy, particularly during and after the turmoil of the First World War. It helped explain the disappointments and fears of a wide range of citizens, not only frustrated reformers and deflated idealists but also anxious business leaders and alarmed cultural conservatives. A representative range of these responses is explored in the remaining chapters of this book.

The response for some was simple denunciation of the propagandistic villains. Others, then as now, went further, urging that concerted educational efforts could save society—whether through enlightened school systems or newly professional journalism. Still others counseled that fire must be fought with fire. The best answer to bad propaganda, some said, was good propaganda. (The only problem was sorting out which was which.)

A few pushed their analysis to more skeptical, even cynical, levels. For them, the problem was that democratic hopes were unreasonable in the first place. Consensual governing systems may have worked in Aristotle's polis or in the old Roman Republic, but they were simply not up to the challenges of extended, complex societies. Plato had prophesized that hyper-democracy would readily lead to tyranny, and as time passed, his prophecy seemed to be coming true. Weimar Germany, in the 1920s, was only the latest example. Somewhat more hopefully, but with a stinging sense of realism, Walter Lippmann in 1922 would take apart the notion that spontaneous "public opinion" could provide a dependable foundation for sensible governing in the modern age.

Even more cynical putdowns of the "people" would also make their way into nihilistic conversations in the years following the First World War. None seemed more extreme (nor more apt in many eyes) than those of the Baltimore skeptic H.L. Mencken. "Democracy," he famously concluded, "is a pathetic belief in the collective wisdom of individual ignorance."

Many felt that those words had come true in the summer of 1920—just after the nominations of two Ohio newspaper publishers for the US presidency. Both were rather undistinguished compromise candidates who emerged slowly from smoke-filled rooms at deadlocked national conventions. Neither fared well when compared to the larger-than-life presidential images of Theodore Roosevelt or Woodrow Wilson.

Mencken reacted in the *Baltimore Sun* of July 26, 1920:

> As democracy is perfected, the office of the president represents, more and more closely, the inner soul of the people. On some great and glorious day, the plain folks of the land will reach their heart's desire at last, and the White House will be occupied by a downright fool and a complete narcissistic moron.

Lippmann's reaction was not as extreme as Mencken's, but it was equally telling. Just after that fall's election, he took leave from his editorship at the *New Republic*, retreated to an isolated village on Long Island, and proceeded to write a landmark book called *Public Opinion*. As this study will later suggest, its message speaks to us with particular relevance a century later. It was written in immediate reaction to the demoralizing election of President Warren Harding.

CHAPTER 2

The Power of Suggestion and the Eclipse of Reason

As confidence in public opinion waned in the early years of the twentieth century, many were caught off guard. The new pessimism contrasted sharply with an exuberant faith in public common sense that had mushroomed in the nineteenth century. That optimistic outlook, initially encouraged by Enlightenment rationalism, had been reinforced by romantic bursts of American exceptionalism as the country followed its manifest destiny westward.

Some committed advocates invoked the Latin words *Vox Populi, Vox Dei* ("The Voice of the People Is the Voice of God"). The phrase had been popularized by reformist Whig Party supporters in eighteenth century England, who often traced it back to the philosopher Alcuin's advice to Charlemagne in the eighth century. What the Whigs neglected to note, however, was that Alcuin had actually been warning Charlemagne to reject this naive idea—the voice of the people was most likely to be the voice of Satan.

The American Founding Fathers had generally shared a deep skepticism about public wisdom. Even as the US Constitution was being drafted in 1787, John Adams warned that just about every democratic experiment in history had committed suicide. He and his colleagues were rebelling against excessive top-down power from the king, of course. But they were also deeply fearful of the dangers from below, from what was frequently called "the mob." James Madison referred to the masses of the people as the "rabble." Alexander Hamilton called the people a "great beast." When Benjamin Franklin was asked in the wake of the Constitutional Convention just what the founders had created at their Philadelphia meetings, he famously replied, "A Republic, if you can keep it." And why might this happy outcome be at risk? he was asked. He responded in words that are less often remembered. "The people, having once tasted the dish of democracy—are always disposed to eat more of it than does them good."

The public had its role to play under the new Constitution, but it was a carefully limited one. Not only would the president be chosen by wise elites in an electoral college (themselves chosen in whatever ways a state legislature might prescribe), but US senators would also be elected by state legislatures and given comfortable six-year terms. The judicial branch would be shaped by the president and the Senate. The idea of independent political parties was anathema to many Founding Fathers, and the idea of popular primary elections was unthinkable.

The essential premise of the Constitution was to avoid excessive power for anyone. The key was a careful system of checks and balances: state versus federal, House versus Senate, legislative versus executive versus judicial, public versus private, common interests versus individual rights.

The right to vote was carefully limited. The people at large could not be counted on. This sense of caution had deep roots. Plato after all had warned that too much democracy leads to tyranny—and Aristotle felt that democracy could only work on a limited local scale, within "the sound of a town crier's voice."

Abraham Lincoln would share much of this outlook. At age twenty-eight he centered his first major address—his Springfield Lyceum speech—on the risk that an emotional mob could enshrine a demagogic leader. America would not be defeated by an outside power, he argued, but it could be toppled by its own irrational public.

Four decades earlier James Madison had taken comfort from his hope that geographic distances could cushion the new government against runaway emotion. The sheer size of the country would prevent any local eruption from easily infecting other communities. Of course, this Madisonian safety net would be badly compromised many decades later by the rise of mass media and still later by internet technologies that can send even the wildest emotions surging in seconds across the country and around the planet.

Madison's geographic safety net has fallen victim to the "death of distance." One contemporary result is that groups of believers on all sides can thrive more easily in their own information bubbles, accepting alternative realities and maintaining that other accounts are fake news. But this is not a new phenomenon.

It is worth noting that propaganda campaigns 100 years ago mostly happened in plain sight—via newspapers and billboards, movies, and then radio. Much of the manipulation that goes on a century later, however, is delivered less visibly via highly targeted email programs, social media postings, and YouTube offerings, making it difficult to evaluate, contextualize, correct, or contest their offerings. (Some internet manipulations are even driven by digital algorithms that can pull impressionable recipients into what some describe as conspiracy-minded "rabbit holes.") But, while today's technologies can be more insidious, the risks were becoming increasingly apparent even a century ago.

FROM CONFIDENCE TO CAUTION TO CYNICISM

The nineteenth century's faith in a reliable public did not dissipate all at once. The word *progress* was widely repeated as a new century dawned; the period, after all, is still called the Progressive Era. Yes, the new challenges were enormous, but so, it was hoped, were the new tools for informing and awakening the public—especially in hands of leaders like Theodore Roosevelt and the muckraking journalists. Even the label "propaganda" was used in a favorable sense at first.

Nonetheless, it steadily became clearer to many analysts that the new mass information tools were not only a potential solution but could also be part of the problem. The word *propaganda* quickly became a pejorative buzzword—and eventually something of a fixation. Yes, we have always had propagandists with us. What was new in the early decades of the twentieth century was that they lost much of their protective coloration.

Harold Lasswell, a leading analyst of propaganda a generation later, posited that much older preoccupations with "folklore," "predestination," cosmic "inevitability" and a society's "permanent soul" had left little room for discussions about human "manipulation" and "premeditation." As the true processes of opinion formation became less obscure, he said, what had once seemed natural and gradual could now seem artificial and arbitrary.

In analyzing the rather sudden emergence of the propaganda phenomenon, two factors deserve particular attention. The first of these factors was psychological, a sharpened awareness that the human mind was moved in considerable measure by irrational forces. The second factor, which will be treated in a subsequent chapter, was sociological, an emerging realization that society as a whole was just too immense and complicated for the public to play a dependable political role.

THE PSYCHOLOGY OF CROWDS

When a young Harvard student named Boris Sidis published his doctoral dissertation in 1898, he asked his noted professor, William James, to write an introduction. The book had a long but compelling title: *The Psychology of Suggestion: A Research into the Subconscious Nature of Man and Society*. In his preliminary essay, James referred to it as "almost" the first considered discussion in English of crowd psychology, adding, "There is probably no more practically important topic to the student of public affairs."

For the first third of the twentieth century, the study of crowd psychology was a hot topic for academic investigation. This essay will mention many of these writers, some European and some American, most of them long forgotten but still worth citing if only to demonstrate the scope and the intensity of the phenomenon.

The honorary surgeon to the king of England, Wilfred Trotter, for example, posited the existence of an overpowering gregarious instinct in his influential 1915 book, *The Instinct of the Herd in Peace and War*. Later that year, another British writer, Sir Martin Conway, published a work with a similar title: *The Crowd in Peace and War*. A memorable review of the Conway book appeared in the new and increasingly influential progressive American magazine the *New Republic*. The no-nonsense reviewer was Harold Stearns:

> Before the war the psychology of the crowd held much the same
> position in public favor as that now occupied by the more intimate

Freudian insight. It was the pampered pet of the popular magazines, a four-leafed cloverfield for snippy generalizers and inspired rhetoricians. Wisdom in the subject was believed to be the result of a hasty reading of Tarde and Le Bon, followed by a determined effort to outdo those gentlemen in vagueness.

It wasn't that the Conway book was a poor book of its kind, Stearns said. "It is just that that particular kind is silly and futile."

Silly and futile it may have been for some, but many who wrote, however vaguely, about "the madness of crowds" pointed to a long history of public irrationality. The excesses of the French Revolution were frequently cited. Sidis mentioned peasant uprisings in the Middle Ages, the Dutch Tulip Mania, the South Sea Bubble, and various religious revivals. E.L. Godkin, the distinguished *Nation* editor, had written vividly about the US Financial Panic of 1873, warning that "a new plague had been sent among men; that there was an impalpable, invisible force in the air, robbing them of their wits, of which philosophy has not yet dreamt." Others would reference the tumult of labor agitation, anarchist and socialist uprisings, and the swelling popularity of the "yellow" press.

Crowd psychologists also drew on a growing body of philosophical comment, climaxing in the recent writings of Friedrich Nietzsche, Henri Bergson, and William James himself. But their most important source of intellectual support was the emerging study of the subconscious mind, just beginning to flower in the work of Sigmund Freud. The esteemed progressive historian James Harvey Robinson summed up the impact of the new research when he described it in 1918 as "one of the most astonishing, far-reaching and perturbing achievements of our day and generation."

What changed when individuals became a group? They became more susceptible to suggestion, melting into a herd or pack that could then be "stampeded," reverting to the state of "children" or "savages." Another British writer, William McDougall, described irrational human instincts as the keys of an organ upon which a skilled artist could play his own compositions.

A University of Iowa professor, G.T.W. Patrick, helped popularize these concerns as early as 1900 in the *Popular Science Monthly*. "The Psychology of Crazes" was his title. The "social mind," he wrote, was a "drag" on civilization, activating the "lower brain centers." In his view, this meant that all group associations were potentially evil; even the Daughters of the American Revolution might someday be transformed from fine individuals into "an uncontrolled mob."

Other commentary quickly turned manic. The very word *popularize* was derived from an ancient Latin word for "butcher," one writer suggested, observing that people assembled in groups had always been seen as depraved and cruel.

Such theories were vigorously disputed, meanwhile, by persistent rationalist writers like Walter Lippmann and John Dewey. The latter, in his important 1922 study *Human Nature and Conduct*, would call this preoccupation with group instincts a "hazy fallacy," one that renamed an effect and called it a cause. What some called instincts he saw as "habits" that could be learned and unlearned. Other thinkers would describe crowd psychology in different ways. Was it hypnosis at work, or mere imitation?" Sidis offered the term *suggestibility*. Stearns called for a cease-fire under the banner of a common denominator such as "the disposition to conform." Lippmann usefully described the chaotic debate this way in 1920:

> James's social selves, Trotter's herd instinct, Freud's censor, Tarde's imitation, McDougall's sympathetic induction, Giddings's consciousness of kind, Sidis's suggestibility are all presumably aimed at about the same target, but where these terms coincide and where they diverge is not easy to discover by reading the books. Sometimes it almost seems as if the psychologists do not read each other's books.

One of the more esoteric debates of the period was between the so-called realist and nominalist schools of social science, echoing medieval disputes about the metaphysical reality of certain abstractions. The realist group included thinkers such as Gustave Le Bon and Scipio Sighele, working in the tradition of Emile Durkheim and Auguste Comte. For them, social groups were organic, and the whole was indeed greater than the sum of its parts. The "group mind" was a reality even though its members might change, said William McDougall, just as a forest is the same forest even though every tree in it might die and be replaced.

On the nominalist side of the ledger were writers such as Franklin Giddings, Charles Ellwood, and James Mark Baldwin, operating, they said, in the tradition of Herbert Spencer and tending to ridicule their metaphysically oriented colleagues. Ellwood, for example, delivered a resounding no in answer to the question "Is Society a Physical Unity?" in the *American Journal of Sociology* in 1905. Lippmann told his readers to put away such "metaphysical ghosts." Later, psychologist Floyd Allport would sum up the nominalist perspective this way: "the individual in the crowd behaves just as he would alone, *only more so!*"

The problem, of course, was that the individual acting alone was not necessarily all that rational a creature to begin with. People had long realized, as some writers reminded their colleagues, that the problem did not lie with the crowd but with human nature. As P.T. Barnum had allegedly put it, "there's a sucker born every minute." The Hearst newspaper's editorial writer, Arthur Brisbane, traced his own views back to the agrarian populist Tom Watson, whose formula for success was to "always remember that it is impossible to exaggerate the stupidity of the public." That sentiment was reinforced just before the Great War when, to the consternation of many, the poor results of US Army IQ tests were announced.

It was hard to deny compelling evidence of public stupidity. But even as these doubts mounted, many would still respond with words they (perhaps inaccurately) ascribed to Abraham Lincoln: "You can fool all of the people some of the time, and some of the people all of the time. But you can't fool all the people all the time." As the nineteenth century proceeded, however, others pointed out that if you could indeed fool all of the people some of the time, and some of the people all of the time, then that could still add up to a heck of a lot of pretty foolish people!

FROM LE BON TO FREUD

The discussion of public irrationality throughout this period owed a great deal to the force and flair of Gustave Le Bon, whose book *The Crowd: A Study of the Popular Mind* was published in Paris in 1895 and in translation in London the next year. It became the most widely translated, reprinted, and cited of all the works on crowd psychology, from that time to the present day.

For Le Bon the crowd constituted the dull base of a pyramid that was topped by the intelligent elite. Shared decision-making could only guarantee error. "On general questions, a vote recorded by forty academicians is no better than that of forty water carriers." Why? Because, by a process of group hypnosis, even the cultivated individual was reduced to "a barbarian, that is a creature acting by instinct." LeBon's great rival, Gabriel Tarde, attributed the same problem to human "imitation." But for Le Bon, "a crowd, doubtless, is always unconscious" and the coming "Era of Crowds" portends "the death of civilization."

For Sidis the answer would mean avoiding the hypnotic spell of group life altogether; for Le Bon the answer was to harness it. For him, trying to reason with a crowd was like trying to talk with a cyclone. Instead of using reasoned argument, the leader must use emotional tools, including the force of prestige. A charismatic hero like Napoleon, by allying himself with elemental forces such as history, race, and culture, could produce "heroic crowds" and thus bring order out of chaos. Le Bon's description would surely have continuing relevance.

Among those who resisted Le Bon's analysis was Sigmund Freud, most explicitly in his *Group Psychology and the Analysis of the Ego*, first published in 1921 and available in English a year later. Building on ideas that had been suggested in his *Totem and Taboo* nine years earlier, Freud dismissed all notions of an organic crowd or a group consciousness, putting aside as well concepts such as hypnotic suggestion, gregarious instincts, imitation, and all the rest. Instead he explained the influence of a leader as the product of an erotic relationship with the public. Yes, an erotic relationship.

The motivating energy that shaped social life, Freud argued, lay within each separate human being. It was essentially selfish. Each individual follower was directing his or her libidinal energy toward a leader, just as the "primal horde" lavished its emotions on the murdered primal father. To be sure, social direction came from leaders at the top of the social pyramid, but the essential energy came from the bottom. The leader's role, effectively, was to seduce the public. At about the same time (in 1922), an article promoting the emerging public relations industry was tellingly entitled: "Keep on a' Courtin' That Girl!"

Group feeling, Freud suggested, had to be marshaled by a common chieftain. When Philip Rieff wrote about Freud many years later, he noted the parallel between Freud's father figure and Big Brother of Orwell's *1984*. The commanding leader was essentially a center around whom disturbed lives could reorganize themselves.

A respected American critic of propaganda in the 1920s, Everett Dean Martin of the Cooper Union, relied on Freudian thinking in his much-cited study *The Behavior of Crowds*. The crowd, he maintained, was a neurotic group, one that is experiencing "a coincident somnambulism." But the galvanizing factor, he emphasized, was the object that is shared by the crowd and not the mental activity itself. "There is no more reason for believing in a collective mind than in a collective stomach."

Freud's theory helped turn the intellectual discussion away from spontaneous, uncontrolled crowds and toward the role of deliberate propagandists. One further implication of this turn was that group behavior, properly led, could also be stable and constructive.

This optimistic approach was compelling for the young Walter Lippmann. In a 1916 *New Republic* book review, he welcomed Wilfred Trotter's biological case for the existence of a strong "gregarious" instinct because it presented gregariousness as a normal impulse, as much to be admired as egoistic desires. An irrational public was not necessarily a pathological one. Arthur Christensen, a Dane, similarly suggested that a raucous crowd could become a positive "culture," possibly even resembling "a tranquil flock of sheep."

Britain's Graham Wallas (of whom we will be hearing a good deal more in the next chapter) had accepted the role of unreason as early as 1908: "To make men think, one must begin by making them to feel," he had offered. Giving the irrational its due and then controlling the result could be the most supremely rational of strategies. But many others were still frightened by the mob's potential. In time, they would cite the evidence of public hysteria during the First World War to refute the contention that a nation could unleash public emotion and still remain in charge of it.

Among others, it was a proudly leftist young intellectual, Randolph Bourne, who led this attack on progressive pragmatism. His descriptions of wartime behavior came directly out of crowd psychology literature; he spoke vividly of the mob, the mass, the herd, the "primitive" and "irresistible" gregarious instinct. A people at war, he would say, reflected "filial mysticism" and a "recrudescence of the child." The result he famously described in the phrase "War is the health of the state."

Bourne's response was to embrace a particularly radical form of individualism. Some pragmatists may have hoped they could control the stampeding beast, but for Bourne it was "difficult to see how the child on the back of a mad elephant is to be any more effective than the child who tries to stop him from the ground." In the end, only the lonely and intelligent individual could save public opinion from "premature crystallization." The duty of the responsible few was to "divide, confuse, disturb, keep the intellectual water constantly in motion to prevent any such ice from ever forming."

So it was that faith in a reasonable public crumbled as the new century stumbled on. Even many who had once honored public reason would slide quickly away, past the pragmatic halfway stations of Wallas or Lippmann or Trotter or Dewey, and into a new pessimism that cowered before the supposed power of propaganda.

POP PSYCHOLOGY JOINS THE CHORUS

The theories of social scientists and philosophers were echoed at the popular level by a faddish obsession of the period. It swept up many who never read a journal article or an academic treatise but were captivated by a host of popular manuals selling the powers of do-it-yourself hypnotism. By invoking the "awesome power of suggestion," people were told how they might control the direction not only of their own minds but also the minds of friends and customers—and perhaps even strangers.

Hypnotic theories had crested in the eighteenth century when an Austrian professor named Anton Mesmer advanced new theories about the power of magnetic currents. He promised that he could use human touch and words to direct these forces inside one's body—and thus cure both physical and emotional ailments. A widespread cult developed—especially among aristocrats in prerevolutionary France, where Mesmer lived after he was driven out of Austria. Mesmer cults gathered evening after evening in Paris for escapist and often hedonistic rituals involving hot water tubs and the linking of human flesh to transport the magnetic waves and their curative powers.

King Louis XVI became so suspicious of this new fad and its threat to established society that he formed an investigative commission to look into it. Made up of leading French scientists, it was chaired by one of the world's most famous scientists, none other than the American ambassador to France, Benjamin Franklin. Franklin's commission found that the whole thing was a hoax and that the cures it claimed were based on human imagination. Of course, just because science reaches a clear conclusion does not mean that people will necessarily buy into that conclusion. Mesmerism—the word, if not the precise theory—continued as an object of at least some public interest well into the nineteenth century, and that interest expanded significantly toward the century's end. (The word "mesmerize," of course, continues in popular use today.)

Contributing to the popularity of Mesmerism was the US appearance in 1894 of George du Maurier's novel *Trilby*. The English writer had first suggested writing about the theme of hypnotic power to his American counterpart Henry James but then followed the latter's advice to undertake the project himself.

The reception for the novel in England had been lukewarm, but the book produced a veritable *Trilby* mania in America. It was serialized in *Harper's Monthly* from January to August 1894 and then published in New York in September, selling over 100,000 copies by December of that year. A stage version opened shortly thereafter, and Trilby parties, Trilby songs, and even Trilby foods blossomed across the country. (A Broadway caterer molded ice cream in the shape of the heroine's celebrated foot.) By the time the fad ended, du Maurier's book had become the best-selling novel in the United States in many years, outdistancing even blockbusters such as *Ben-Hur* and *Looking Backward*.

The novel (which a number of future leaders in the media world, including Edward Bernays, read in childhood) would become a reference point for those who later wrote or talked about the hypnotizing potentials of propaganda. Commentators would routinely describe a charismatic leader as "a regular Svengali," referring to the mesmerist at the center of du Maurier's story. As late as 1941, Judy Garland and Mickey Rooney were still singing about Trilby and Svengali in the popular Hollywood musical *Babes on Broadway*.

Du Maurier's Svengali was a repugnant individual, reflecting the worst of anti-Semitic prejudices. His words "were pronounced with a Hebrew-German accent, and uttered in his hoarse, rasping, nasal throaty rook's caw, his big yellow teeth baring themselves in a mongrel canine snarl, his heavy eyelids drooping over his insolent black eyes." Yet he could exert a power over others that was mysterious and absolute, "dark" and "oriental." His victim was the young heroine Trilby, naturalistic, pure, uneducated, blond, and Occidental. He transformed her into a great concert singer, even as he replaced her will with his own. His hypnotic power, it should be remembered, was assumed by many readers to bear at least some scientific validation.

With a single word Svengali could turn the vital beauty into

> an unconscious Trilby of marble, who could produce wonderful sounds—just the sounds he wanted, and nothing else—and think his thoughts and wish his wishes—and love him at his bidding with strange unreal factitious love, just his own love for himself turned inside out.

What explained the power? Trilby's friend Laird knew all too well:

> He mesmerized you; that's what it is—mesmerism! I've often heard of it, but never seen it done before. They get you into their power, and just make you do any blessed thing they please—like, murder, steal— anything! And kill yourself into the bargain when they're done with you! It's just too terrible to think of.

Excited and impressionable youngsters across America would soon be repeating the mesmerist's famous words again and again (and for many years later) in backyard conversations: "And you shall see nothing, hear nothing, think of nothing but Svengali, Svengali, Svengali!"

Just as people saw propaganda everywhere once they had a word for it, so they saw Svengalis everywhere once they had a name for him. He became the very image of the evil propagandist, someone who could actually fool most of the people most of the time. The Trilby craze helped create, for a while at least, a sinister connotation for the very concept of psychological analysis. One plumbed the subconscious not to discover a truer self but rather to locate a mechanism for the displacement of the self by the will of another.

No shortage of opportunists rushed in to exploit the craze. One X. LaMotte Sage, a professor at Central College in Sedalia, Missouri, assured "everybody" in an 1897 tract called *Hypnotism as It Is: A Book for Everybody* that he would teach them to get around the "sentinels of the mind" of their neighbors. A certain William Barnes included a chapter entitled "Suggestion as an Aid to Business Men, Solicitors and Salespeople" in his 1900 book *Psychology, Hypnotism, Personal Magnetism and Clairvoyance*. A minister named Stanley LeFevre Krebs added his view in 1901 that the miracles of Jesus in fact resulted from "indirect suggestion" and that one who followed in his steps could also become "a master of the mind" and a "king" of public consciousness. In the same year, one R. Osgood Mason warned that religious revivalists and advertisers were, in fact, abusing the constructive potentials of the hypnotic process.

It is worth recalling as well how another popular literary creation of the age paralleled the Trilby story. George Bernard Shaw's *Pygmalion* in 1912 told of a near-miraculous transformation of a bedraggled Cockney flower girl into someone who could pass for a duchess, though in Shaw's play it was Henry Higgins's phonetics skills that did the trick. But in both stories, the essential implication was that those who possessed special knowledge could transform the pliable consciousness of others.

The emerging advertising industry also began to speak in the language of suggestion and hypnosis. The most important influence in this development was that of Walter Dill Scott, a professor of psychology (and later president) at Northwestern University. Scott's writings—particularly *The Theory of Advertising* in 1904, *The Psychology of Public Speaking* in 1907, and *The Psychology of Advertising* in 1908—were the first in the field, and for many years they were the best studies available of an important applied science.

Scott had trained originally to be a Presbyterian mission teacher in China, but he abandoned those plans in order to study in Germany with Wilhelm Wundt, a pioneering psychology scholar. He was taken with Wundt's concept of a "wach hypnosis," a narrowing of consciousness under certain stimuli, suggesting that the first step of a leader should not be "to convince or sway the crowd, but to create it."

By 1915 the Harvard psychologist Hugo Munsterberg was describing hypnotism itself as a purer form of salesmanship. In 1916 he published a study of motion pictures, blaming them for an increase in crime and attributing their influence to an "incomparable intensity" that "heightened suggestibility," producing a "one-sided propaganda." A widely traveled Toledo lawyer, Gustavus Ohlinger, also wrote of propaganda hypnosis in conspiratorial terms, warning that the Germans had been "Prussianizing" American schools for years. What's more, he added, "so completely had we been hypnotized by the prestidigitations of Kultur that these obtrusions in our school books were not even noticed until after the war had aroused us from our trance." Meanwhile, journalists who earlier had been criticized for wielding the power of sensationalism now were attacked for using the power of suggestion.

A prolific student of propaganda in the 1920s, George Sylvester Viereck (often a pro-German writer—even into the 1930s), also described the propagandist as a master hypnotist. A

1930s writer using the pseudonym V.F. Calverton linked propaganda directly to the "hypnotic compulsion" of Svengali in a *Scribner's Magazine* piece that he called "Our Hypnotized World."

And then along came auto-suggestion. Its most conspicuous advocate was a Frenchman, Emile Coue, one of the best-selling authors of the interwar period. "Suggestion of suggestion; all is suggestion" was his motto. An American student of Coue, Frederick Pierce, described the mass suggestion process as "human engineering," lecturing before advertising clubs across the country. One of his books was entitled *Mobilizing the Mid-Brain*.

Others joined the mounting chorus. Names such as George Beard, Phineas P. Quimby, Orison S. Marden, and Yogi Rumacharaka became familiar to self-help readers throughout the United States, the latter using as his title *The Psychology of Salesmanship*. James Alexander, in a 1924 book entitled *Thought Control in Everyday Life*, advised his anxious readers to repeat this mantra daily: "I am not going to allow anything that I read to harm me or to have any power over me."

In 1918, the same year in which he was elected president of the American Psychological Association, Joseph Jastrow published a critical appraisal of the "kingdom of unreason." He traced the roots of the mind-over-matter movement back to William James, included Christian Science in his critique, and described the propaganda phenomenon as an extreme form of the "will to believe."

A comprehensive history of hypnotism by Robert W. Marks in 1947 extended the analysis. "Social hypnosis," he charged, can turn people into

> primeval zombies reverting mechanically and instinctually to the social pattern of the fang and the claw. ... The same mechanism which makes for flagpole sitting and goldfish swallowing and which sends schoolgirls into fainting spells at the sound of Sinatra's voice may under other conditions send them into the gas chambers of concentration camps.

The only answer for Marks, as for Sidis and Bourne, lay in an anarchic individualism in which people would avoid even casual club memberships in order to remain "free unaffiliated individualists, ... unaffected by winds of enchantment which blow ancient blood lusts from archaic caves."

The "winds of enchantment" with their "ancient blood lusts" frightened many. To be sure, the hypnosis and mind-cure manuals also presented their insights as instruments for achieving a better life. But those who looked on from a public-interest perspective generally shared the reaction of Trilby's friend Laird when he concluded that the prospects of control through suggestion were "just too terrible to think of."

CHAPTER 3

The Erosion of Community in a Distended Society

T he vulnerability of the subconscious mind was by no means a new discovery in the early years of the twentieth century, nor was its potential for
disrupting democracy. But why then did its threat, at a moment of renewed
progressive energy, suddenly seem much more ominous? Why did so many
observers look at the once revered public and begin to see the ominous
crowd? Many analysts explained the development by pointing to an enormous
sociological change.

What they identified was a change in the very nature of social relations, a
stretching and snapping of the ties that had disciplined human interactions when
communities were more compact and personal. Related to the growing skepticism
concerning human rationality, this transformation of social realities becomes for
our analysis the second great factor that undermined faith in the sovereign public
as a new century began. Some early observers would portray this development
as a matter of social disorganization. Historian Robert Wiebe characterized it in
1966 as the erosion of community in "The Distended Society," a term that usefully
embraces the concepts of both extension and distortion.

A host of analysts, then and since, some well-known and some now obscure, outlined similar explanations. What follows here is a sampling of their observations.

Graham Wallas, who from his British base had outlined so well the challenges
of unreason in 1908, described the distension phenomenon in a landmark book
published in 1914. The title he gave to the book and to the reality it described was
The Great Society (with the word *great* implying a quantitative rather than a qual-
itative judgment). In the preface to his first chapter, Wallas cited none other than
Woodrow Wilson:

> Yesterday and ever since history began, men were related to
> one another as individuals. ... Today the everyday relationships
> of men are largely with impersonal concerns, with organizations,
> not with other individuals. Now this is nothing short of a new age
> of human relationships, a new stage-setting for the drama of life.

Wilson had aptly summed it up in a single word: what had happened, he said, was the "delocalization" of social life.

For Wallas, this change in social scale demanded a new emphasis on decentralized decision-making. Restoring the influence of thoughtful public discussion should be the goal. "The newspaper," he complained, "is taking to a large extent the place of conversation … without securing that which is its essential value as an intellectual instrument, the stimulus of one mind by free association with another." His initial problem with the new mass media was that it was not interactive, although the Twitter and Facebook threads of a later age may not have reassured him about the advantages of interactive exchanges.

The influential American sociologist Charles Horton Cooley had anticipated Wallas, describing the new social reality as "the age of diffusion." A rampant "superficiality" in human contact was "the central fact" in the history of his time. The risk, Cooley worried, was that the power of suggestion would be magnified as settled habits dissolved and traditional structures had "gone to pieces."

For Cooley, as for Wallas, the mass-distributed daily newspaper symbolized the problem, inscribed with "world-wide gossip" and threatening the ideal of face-to-face communication, even as it screened husband from wife at the family breakfast table. (Randolph Bourne described the same phenomenon—although he welcomed the change as one that would liberate the autonomous individual.)

H.G. Wells's analysis agreed with Wilson: "We are delocalized." Similarly, John Dewey blamed the "era of bunk" on what he called the "remoter world." The "cake of custom" had grown "flat and soggy," he said; the realm of "shared experience" on which order with freedom depends had almost disappeared. "The machine age," wrote the man from the Vermont village, "in developing the Great Society has invaded and partially disintegrated the small communities of former times without generating a Great Community." That was the heart of the problem, one which has grown more severe over time.

In a simpler time, the process of opinion formation had retained a mystical, natural, quality. What was missing now was an older sense of shared history in the small community, where one knew the subtleties of language and the ways of those who used it, where a word or glance could communicate a greater store of meaning, and where people had a better sense of just whom they could trust. In such a world, with the aid of largely intuitive strategies, consensus could emerge.

In the great, distended, remote, and delocalized society, all of this was changed. Where discussion had been efficient, it now could seem inelastic, nonreciprocal, and even contrived. One's new counselors were often strangers, a new breed of publicists who were now compared to the circus and carnival promoters of an earlier day, ephemeral agents who popped in and out of community life

The pioneering German sociologist Ferdinand Toennies suggested that *Gesellschaft* had replaced *Gemeinschaft*. Another German writer of the 1920s acutely attributed the power of propaganda to the inability of social assemblies "to keep up with social extension." His name was Adolph Hitler.

What was happening to the personal culture of small communities was not so different from what had happened in ancient Greece when Socrates mourned the decline of intimate, trustworthy oral exchange in the face of a potentially impersonal new technology. The new technology that Socrates had been worried about was called writing.

Canadian scholar Harold Innis some years later described a narrowing of the range from which material originates and a widening of the range of reception. The student-teacher ratio had been altered. Moreover, to continue the comparison, classroom hours had been radically shortened; the time available to most people for digesting information was a fraction of what it once had been.

As the size of relevant audiences was extended, a new class of statisticians produced chilling analyses of the public's predictability—and by implication, the public's manipulability. A writer (Frederick Dwight) in the *Yale Review* in 1909 attributed the new power of advertising to a weakening of community commitments, something that also explained, as he saw it, the new unaligned vote and the climbing divorce rate.

An important new voice in this discussion was that of Edward Ross, a highly visible and decidedly controversial sociologist and criminologist, who talked as early as 1896 about something that he termed "the Big Society." He pursued this idea in his notable book called *Social Control* in 1901. "If the molecules of the local group are jarred asunder," he wrote, "it is partly because they fall under influences which make them vibrate in faster unisons."

For the early Ross the expansion of relevant audiences could help save democracy by broadening public discussion. "It is easy to poison a well," he declared, "but to poison the dew—that is quite another thing." By 1907, however, Ross had changed course, giving up on the commercial press and suggesting that an endowed press might be more responsible. He had come to realize that even the dew might be contaminated. In a book that he revealingly called *Sin and Society: An Analysis of Latter Day Iniquity,* Ross described the public in certain moods as "a stupid, flushed giant at bay." In his notable *Social Psychology* the next year, he blamed the dangers of irrational crowds on the fact that "mental touch is no longer bound up with physical proximity."

Eager to help remedy the problem, Ross urged a renewal of family life, the creation of city parks and recreational facilities, a more determined inculcation of tradition mores, and even (in a stance that later brought pronounced public calumny) resistance to what he saw as the dangers of racial assimilation.

NEW TECHNIQUES AND NEW TECHNICIANS

As social distension expanded, so did the potential autonomy of the leader. The servant of the public would be first its informer, next its educator, then its leader, and eventually its master. Public consent, once seen as the hopeful alternative to coercion, was now seen as something that itself might be coerced.

And this new set of social realities would work to transform many fields of endeavor: advertising, religion, social service, and political campaigning, among others.

One critical moment came in December 1901 when Walter Dill Scott was invited to lecture at Chicago's Agate Club on the psychology of advertising. In that path-breaking lecture and the book that emerged from it, Scott suggested that the industry's familiar role as a broker of newspaper space was a stale one and that bold new thinking was needed.

Just two years later, and only a few blocks away from the Agate Club, the new head of the advertising firm of Lord and Thomas pondered the same topic. "What is advertising?" Albert Lasker kept asking himself and his colleagues. A prospective employee, John E. Kennedy, heard of Lasker's inquiry, came to his office building, and from a downstairs saloon sent word that he could answer the query in three words. Lasker called him in and growled, "I am hungry. What are these three words?"

"Salesmanship in print," replied Kennedy.

For the rest of his legendary career, Lasker referred to that moment as a turning point not only for his own thinking but for the industry as whole. The thought seems like a commonplace concept today. But for Lasker and for many others, it seemed a new insight. The personal arts of the salesman, traditionally exercised orally, could also be used by those who employed written words though the mass media. The salesman would no longer have to go house to house.

Advertising, seen in this light, could offer a great deal more than mere information. With Scott, Lasker, Kennedy, and Lasker's chief copywriter, Claude Hopkins, leading the way, the mushrooming ad industry discovered the power and profitability of propaganda. (In 1920 Lasker himself would become the central strategist in Warren Harding's successful presidential campaign.) Nor was it surprising that young advertising professionals would play key roles with the wartime Committee on Public Information.

Religious revivalists shared in the fervor, and in the realization that new social realities required an extensive use of new communication tools. Because the Holy Ghost was the validator of what they were saying, they were happy to discuss the techniques by which they helped the Divinity produce a desired effect. The response they sought also had to be achieved quickly, particularly in the case of itinerant revivalists. Accordingly, they openly embraced a wide range of nonrational appeals and delocalized techniques.

It is worth recalling that the term *propaganda* first achieved prominence in a respected religious context. The religious parallel would be cited in a book by one future propagandist, claiming that he actually had learned about controlling mass sentiment from the experience of the church. The book was *Mein Kampf*, and the writer, again, was Adolph Hitler.

In America the dominant religious model was not Roman Catholicism but frontier Calvinism. The appeals of Jonathan Edwards, the manuals of Charles Grandison Finney, and the impressive example of Dwight Moody provided early American instruction in the arts of crowd psychology. The most popular model for emerging American propagandists in the new twentieth century was the evangelist Billy Sunday. Two of the most prominent publicists of the day, Ivy Lee and George Creel, cited Sunday as a prototype. *Billy Sundayism* became a popular term, and Sunday was one of the models for Elmer Gantry, the prototypical antihero for the novelist Sinclair Lewis.

One example of Sunday's emotional rhetoric is a prayer he delivered in the House of Representatives during the First World War: "Thou knowest, oh Lord, that no nation so infamous, vile, greedy, sensuous, bloodthirsty, ever disgraced the pages of history. Make bare thy mighty arm, oh Lord, and smite the hungry wolfish Hun, whose fangs drip with blood." It was the only prayer in memory, we are told, that caused the House of Representatives to break into applause.

Helen Woodward, the most famous woman in advertising in the 1920s, also cited the religious revivalists as her models. Even when the product was less inspiring, she nonetheless found renewed energy in the sheer passionate fun of being able to convert people. The effectiveness of the message, she also suggested, counts less on its content than on the techniques of the messenger.

Other enthusiastic publicists also invoked religious precedents. The advertising mogul Bruce Barton's model was Jesus Christ himself. Similarly, Herbert Croly (a founder of the *New Republic*) told political leaders that they should emulate Jesus's skill at welding mass morale. Indeed, when a later evangelist, Billy Graham, was described as a "psychologist" in London in 1966, he responded by comparing his psychological techniques to those of not only of Winston Churchill but of Jesus and Paul before him.

The influential Norwegian economist Thorstein Veblen bitterly compared the newly visible advertising professionals to religious evangelists, "publicity-agents of the faith." They "promise much and deliver a minimum," commanding "unreasoning assent or acclamation." In a similar vein, H.L. Mencken would compare the typical daily newspaper to "a Baptist evangelist," even while Colonel McCormack's *Chicago Tribune* compared its own role to that of a parish priest.

Mainstream religious leaders, meanwhile, were also becoming aware of new marketing methodologies that could advance their work. One prominent example was the superintendent of the Department of Church and Labor for the Presbyterian Church, Charles Stelzle. He forthrightly began to write about what he called "church advertising," "aggressive evangelism," and "social publicity." The church's outreach efforts should include signs and billboards, leaflets, pamphlets, books, door-to-door canvasses, and above all, placing constant pressures on the secular press. "Every political party" uses these techniques, he observed, and "if it pays for them, it will pay the church." By the time he wrote his memoirs (called *Promotion and Publicity*) in 1926, he was even more convinced that "more things are wrought by publicity than this world dreams of."

A similar message came from John J. Burke, writing in the *Catholic World* in May 1910. He was impressed, he said, by "the great world-wide, trumpet-voiced organ of publicity," emphasizing that "the great victories of publicity have been won by the voice of the few that appealed to the many."

Advocates in other fields would quickly join the parade. As Edward Bernays would write in 1928, "The leaders in social service were among the first consciously to utilize propaganda in the modern sense." In 1910, for example, John A. Kingsbury, assistant secretary of the New York State Charities Aid Association, had put the case quite bluntly:

> Publicity that pulls is publicity that pays, and you must pay for public-
> ity that pulls. ... We must learn from the patent medicine man. ... The
> nature and scope of such publicity, within the bounds of truth and
> morality, should be limited only by its ability to get results.

If critics complained that you have become "a little yellow in your methods," then Kingsbury would candidly declare "that yellow is the color of prophylaxis." Kingsbury's successor made the same argument in the *Annals* in 1916, while the *American Journal of Public Health* complained about the timidity of many public health professionals and recommended the books of Walter Dill Scott.

Other not-for-profit organizations joined in the embrace. The National Child Labor Committee was one; the educational establishment was another. Vera Whitehouse, who first exhibited her publicity talents as chair of the women's suffrage movement in New York State, later applied her skills as a key official in the Committee on Public Information. To a greater degree than has been generally appreciated, it was men and women from a nonprofit background who joined in selling Liberty Bonds, supporting the Red Cross and marshaling public support for the Great War.

A leading recent chronicler of the history of public relations, Scott Cutlip, describes a breakthrough moment in 1901, when Charles Sumner Ward and Lyman L. Pierce launched a publicity campaign to raise millions of dollars for the YMCA. In 1907 the National Tuberculosis Association inaugurated the first of its Christmas Seal campaigns. Evart Routzahn, who helped design that effort, later turned the Russell Sage Foundation into a leading center of social service publicity. Routzahn and his wife, Mary Swain, became a prolific source of writings on the topic, calling for "some quick ready method of spreading information that will arouse public interest in necessary reform." The Community Chest movement joined the party with its first campaign in Cleveland in 1913. By the early 1920s, the president of Harvard University, A. Lawrence Lowell, was recalling how a small body of specialists had developed "the art of exciting enthusiasm by contagion," organizing "a competitive zeal for giving more largely than people really want to give," then as now an understandable objective for a college president.

PROPAGANDISTS AGAINST PROPAGANDA

Perhaps the most visible publicity mavens of the time were the so-called muckrakers, campaigning for reform via journalistic exposés. Surprising as it may seem, however, they did not see themselves as leaders, revivalists, agitators, or anything more than informers of the public. In fact, they were militant critics of business publicists who worked, in their view, to poison opinion. Samuel Hopkins Adams led the assault on patent medicine advertising, for example. Ida Tarbell exposed Standard Oil propaganda; others described the unsavory efforts of the insurance industry to influence the press.

One of the leading muckrakers, Ray Stannard Baker, focused national attention on the railroads' publicity bureaus as gigantic conspiracies to misinform. They constituted, he said in 1906, an "efficient and intelligent machine, capitalizing on new social patterns." His diagnosis rings true today:

> The people, however vigorous their demands for reform, are undisciplined and unorganized. They are torn by petty local interests and they are busy. To make the giant bestir himself the issues must be made very clear and the feeling must be deep. By presenting new information, new issues, new arguments, it is therefore evident that a publicity organization may either convince or confuse public opinion so that it does not settle upon definite demands and stick to them until reforms are attained.

Baker's hope was that mere facts "piled up to the point of dry certitude" could still save democracy from the distractions of fake news.

Just a month before Baker's story appeared, *McClure's Magazine*, the central organ of the muckraking movement, carried an editorial with what was at the time a startling title: "Manufacturing Public Opinion." It helped fix a sinister image for commercial publicity as it described how corporations were setting up "well-equipped, secret departments" for this purpose. But, significantly, it also maintained that merely to expose these machinations would effectively end them! Revelation would itself produce reform.

The fact of the matter was that the muckrakers were also part of an efficient opinion-making machine. They were doing the same thing to business publicists that the business publicists were doing when they described the muckrakers as "propagandists." The concept of propaganda, in sum, had already become a great propaganda tool in its own right. The response to those who framed someone as a framer was to frame them right back. Sound familiar?

Ironically, perhaps, the reformer who pioneered in the self-aware use of political propaganda was not a muckraker but rather the man who gave the muckrakers their name. That, of course, was Theodore Roosevelt. He was "the master press agent of all time," said one of the journalists who covered him regularly, and another added that Roosevelt was "the greatest publicity promoter among the sons of man today." Other progressive politicians followed Roosevelt's lead.

The new tools, however, did not always work so well. And their overt nature was demoralizing to many Progressives. In 1915 the *New Republic* reflected some of their frustrated idealism in words that sound remarkably similar to twenty-first century discussions of a post-fact, post-truth society.

> Today we allow public opinion to grow up like a slum child, untended, disregarded, the victim of every money-seeking adventurer. We permit it to be turned against itself, to be misled with false news, published for profit. What we need is not censorship or suppression, but a positive antibody against falsehood and stupidity. We need some means of educating the adult mind, perhaps some Public Defender of the truth. ... The problem in this country is to develop through popular discussion a steady, sane, tolerant, selfreliant public opinion, organized nationally, yet free from jingoism, and above the level of mere mob mind.

As world war approached, faith in public opinion was fading quickly among progressive leaders. Their concern was deeply reinforced with the coming of the Great War in the West and with the Russian Revolution in the East. V.I. Lenin, throughout his writings, had explicitly condemned publicity in order to herald propaganda. The totalitarian potential of propaganda was becoming more evident to all.

As the stakes rose in this period, leading liberal thinkers such as Herbert Croly, Walter Lippmann, and Walter Weyl worried increasingly about the newly impersonal society, sometimes even admitting that meaningful leadership in a distended society might actually have to compromise old norms of democratic consent. Weyl was typical, hoping in 1912 that the public might eventually grow to a new "level of democratic striving" but also recognizing, for the moment at least, that more active leadership was needed and that the voice of the people could no longer be relied upon as the voice of God.

***

Both psychologically and sociologically, Americans saw their world change dramatically in the early 1900s. As similar changes confront another rapidly changing century, their reactions can have continuing relevance.

The chapters that lie ahead tell the stories of six thoughtful individuals who wrestled personally and institutionally with these difficult changes. Two, Ivy Lee and Edward Bernays, are widely considered to be the founding fathers of the public relations profession. Two others, George Creel and Woodrow Wilson, were at the epicenter of the country's most extensive propaganda exercise during the First World War. Finally, two additional voices, John Dewey and Walter Lippmann, helped shape an influential intellectual response to the challenges of their new information environment. For different reasons, all six of these voices are still worth listening to.

CHAPTER 4

Ivy Lee

The Patrician Propagandist

Almost every history of the public relations industry in America lists Ivy Lee as its first "professional" practitioner. He publicized himself that way, distinguishing his role as a "counselor" in the field from others who were normally described as press agents. But Lee's worldview predated the emergence of his profession; he was a traditional nineteenth century gentleman pioneering in a decidedly twentieth century occupation. His life and work provide a useful perspective on how new media realities challenged long-established habits of political thought.

George A. Parker was a press agent of the old school, a colorful political warhorse in five Democratic presidential campaigns. He had the contacts to get news stories sidelined; he knew the tricks that could win an extra headline. He left the Democratic National Committee after the 1904 election and opened the nation's first public relations firm. As his partner, Parker, fifty-seven, took on a young man of just twenty-seven years named Ivy Ledbetter Lee.

Lee was a child of both the Old and the "New" South. His father, James Wideman Lee, was a circuit preacher of the Methodist Episcopal church; his mother, Emma Eufala Ledbetter, was the daughter of a prominent Methodist minister. Emma was thirteen years old when Ivy was born in 1877.

James Wideman Lee became a prominent Atlanta minister in the 1880s. He was a popular preacher and a crusader for racial and religious understanding. One of his pet crusades was the reconciliation of evolution and Christianity. Another of his causes was the New South economic development movement. He spoke at the funeral of the movement's most prominent leader, Henry Grady. Young Ivy Lee took Grady as his hero. And he also came to admire a different kind of southerner, the folklorist Joel Chandler Harris, who entertained the Lee children with warm tales of antebellum plantation life.

From all of these influences, Ivy Lee learned to admire the power of language, sharpening his verbal skills as a school debater. After two years at Emory University, he entered Princeton University in 1896, where he wrote for the *Princetonian* and came to know a popular professor named Woodrow Wilson. He would remember warmly in later years his long countryside walks with Wilson. He entered Harvard Law School in 1898 but was soon forced to leave when he ran out of money.

Lee arrived in New York in 1899 (with $5.25 in his pocket), did the rounds as a reporter under Hearst, Ochs, and Pulitzer, and met Parker working on political campaigns. But the world of headlines and sensations did not appeal to Lee. He came to admire, instead, men of the solid establishment, with their grand homes, fine food, and good company. Some of his happiest moments would come when his family was listed in the *Social Register* and when his daughter made her social debut in 1926 at the Court of St. James. His tastes by that time had come to include private railroad cars, Gothic cathedrals, and grand opera.

Celebrity itself dazzled Lee. As a teenager he wrote to well-known personalities, keeping their replies in a prized scrapbook. At Princeton he inspired a playful class prophecy in the school yearbook, the *Nassau Herald*, one that pictured him carrying a book entitled *Great Men Who Have Met Me* and humming a song of his own composition entitled "Only Me, Ivy Lee."

In later life, his son reported, Lee made a science out of joining the right private clubs around the world. He once reprimanded a business associate, "You spend too much time with unimportant people."

And so it was that these two men came together in 1904 to create the firm of Parker and Lee: one the puffer, the press agent, the puller of wires, the other an aspiring mover and shaker in a potentially elegant new profession of public relations.

Lee insisted from the start that he was a full-fledged business advisor, comparing himself not to the journalist he had briefly been but to the lawyer he had wanted to become. He would go on to persuade the most eminent men of his time that his techniques could serve their interests. Here lay his claim to the title of pioneer. The way in which American business came to regard publicity was deeply influenced by Lee's approach. More than anyone else, he sold publicity to the establishment.

His first important customer, in 1906, was George Baer, head of the embattled coal mine operators. He joined the Pennsylvania Railroad management in 1908 and advised the Rockefeller family from 1914 until his death in 1934. Along the way, the American Petroleum Institute, the Copper and Brass Research Association, the Trans-Atlantic Passenger Conference, and the Cotton-Textile Institute would all hire his services. A host of corporations did so too: among them Bethlehem Steel, Armour and Company, the American Tobacco Company, and the Chrysler Corporation. He also advised a host of prominent New York banks, as well as foreign businesses and governments.

His nonbusiness clients were also prestigious, including the Red Cross, Riverside Memorial Church, the Cathedral of St. John the Divine, and Harvard and Princeton Universities. He was a director of the Metropolitan Opera Company and chaired a fund-raising committee for the American Historical Association. He counseled on the development of Colonial Williamsburg and is credited with first suggesting the publication of the *William and Mary Quarterly*.

Lee was not, on the other hand, very interested in show business or politics, although he served a few well-established clients with familiar show business names like like Zukor, Lasky, DeMille, United Artists, and the American Society of Composers, Authors, and Publishers (ASCAP). He helped arrange the triumphal national tours of both Richard Byrd and Charles Lindbergh and consulted on the presidential campaign of John Davis in 1924.

Lee's sumptuous offices were said to be one of the few places in New York where millionaires regularly were kept waiting. Here he helped teach his clients to cope with a newly boisterous and distended public.

PUBLIC SOVEREIGNTY: KEEPING THE FAITH

Lee's nineteenth century upbringing taught him that public sovereignty was the keystone of American life. Faith in the public closely resembled religious faith—widely shared, rooted in mystery, and often resistant to empirical analysis. Lee came to see himself as an evangelist for that faith. Through the arts of publicity, he could help protect the sacred public from those who would abuse it. He could thus help advance a new day of social harmony.

As others talked increasingly about the irrational crowd, he affirmed with growing vehemence his faith in a sensible public and the importance of sharing information that would give his ideal public a chance to regroup. His constituents agreed. Theodore Vail, the dominant telephone executive who had helped popularize the term *public relations* even before 1910, suggested in 1915 that publicity would bring "the millennium." Samuel Insull, leader of the electric power industry, and John McGraw of the McGraw-Hill publishing firm were similarly exuberant. The latter's influential publication, the *Electric Railway Journal*, declared in 1916 that fostering good public relations was the most important topic it had covered over the past decade.

Many, their names long since forgotten, wrote in agreement. A.J. Eddy, a Chicago lawyer, praised the prospect that frankness would replace concealment as a central competitive technique. Henry Clews saw publicity as an extension of Social Darwinism; secrecy (as Wilson also argued) had been "the defense of the weak." D.F. Wilcox argued that the role of information was to "control the state through the authority of facts."

"It is practically assumed here," a scholar had written in the second issue of the *American Journal of Sociology* in 1895, "that whenever the people express themselves on any question they are right. The people cannot make a mistake." It may not always be apparent to everyone, the article continued, but in the end, collective opinion deserved its sovereign role.

Reinforcing the authority of public opinion was the fact that it was so surpassingly ill-defined. For Locke and Jefferson, it had been nothing less than Nature's chosen voice. President Abbott Lawrence Lowell of Harvard liked to call it "the sober second sense of the people." James Russell Lowell compared it to the invisible pressure of the atmosphere. Robert Park and Ernest W. Burgess called it "a form of social weather." Woodrow Wilson identified it as the unseen "atmosphere of every government."

A few decades earlier, US president James Garfield had lavishly shared his own faith that public wisdom would emerge in the end from "four million Republican firesides, where the thoughtful voters, with wives and children about them, with the calm thoughts inspired by love of home and country, with the history of the past, the hopes of the future, and knowledge of the great men who have adorned and blessed our nation in days gone by."

In a similarly mystical vein, Senator Robert La Follette would later offer comfort to those who were appalled by the world war hysteria. "Sometimes it sleeps," he allowed, "sometimes it seems the sleep of death; but, sir, the sovereign power of the people never dies." Again, his faith was rooted in nature.

> In the agricultural districts, where the day is spent by the farmer following his plow or his harvester, mixing his thinking with his work, in the quiet and hush of country life, where the blast of the bugle and the roll of the drum is not disturbing the serenity, there is a wiser judgment, a truer test.

As late as 1933, the University of Chicago philosopher T.V. Smith echoed the sentiment in no uncertain terms. Some may doubt or fear the voice of the people, he wrote, but "those who have heard it in vast open spaces or in lofty ancestral halls report it as neither nasal nor querulous, but symphonic and full-bodied like the rising and the ceasing of some exquisite folk melody."

Walter Lippmann had summed up this grandiloquent worldview with a pointed critique in his *Public Opinion* in 1922:

> They had a pale god, but warm hearts, and in the doctrine of popular sovereignty they found the answer to their need of an infallible origin for the new social order. There was the mystery, and only enemies of the people touched it with profane and curious hands.

Such then was the climate of opinion within which Ivy Lee would work and write. He would fervently embrace a new force, deliberate publicity, while insisting that he was still playing by old laissez-faire rules. He was by no means alone. Like so many others who pioneered in the public relations field, Lee was reluctant to admit that public information, the great, traditional tool for reconciling knowledgeable leadership with public sovereignty, could also be used to reshape the public and end its sovereign rule.

A RISING BUT REASONABLE PUBLIC

"The people versus the interests" was the great drama of public life as Lee's career took off. Whatever they might piously say about the ultimate virtue of the public, business leaders were inclined to see the public of the immediate moment in a different light. What they came to call "the crowd" could be irrational and unpredictable, a phenomenon to damn and forget about. Lee understood, however, that this less dependable public could not be ignored much longer. The gulf between the people and the interests would have to be bridged. What made his counsel so agreeable, however, was his conviction that the necessary reconciliation could largely take place on business terms. The rise of the people need not jeopardize established conservative values.

What was imperative, in his view, was that business viewpoints should be explained reasonably. Business advocates need not turn themselves into circus barkers. Lee liked to cite Montaigne's incisive sixteenth century suggestion that when the facts were known, sentiment would not be divided. Benjamin Franklin's words also became a useful credo: "When truth and error have fair play, the former is always an overmatch for the latter."

Lee's message from the start was both appealing and attention getting. We are living in a new age of democracy. The crowd is on the march. The old order must yield to the new. Such language had been part of the very air Lee breathed in the New South of the 1880s.

"The crowd is in the saddle," he declared in 1916. The people are the "fountain of all power." Nor was this some passing "evanescent" fad. One of his favorite quotations—he reprinted it in the upper left-hand corner of the newsletter he issued regularly from 1918 to 1933—was from Abraham Lincoln: "Public sentiment is everything," it began. "With public sentiment nothing can fail; without it nothing can succeed."

Lee liked to say that publicity should not be used as a bandage to cover a sore spot but as an antiseptic to clean it and "reveal it to the doctor, which is the public." Another useful metaphor compared the publicist to a clear glass window. "I just raised the curtains and let the people look in." Good publicity, he insisted, "is neither subtle nor mysterious, nor clever. It is honest, direct, and simple, transparent and neutral, shaping communication only by preventing distortion." And even though many clients "shook in their shoes at the teaching" (as one reporter noted), he continued to proclaim that "secrecy is the parent of suspicion."

He had hammered this theme home throughout his career. "Let the people know, and if you are right, you will win," he declared in 1916. A compilation of his writings in 1925 called *Publicity; Some of the Things It Is and Is Not* insisted that "the man who lies to the people is always found out. A million eyes wait to catch him." He liked to talk about the "rugged Anglo-Saxon common sense" of the American people. If they really understood the facts, he said, the people would be fair. Shortly before his death in 1934, he suggested that the public had a mysterious sixth sense that would always detect the truth. The people would always insist on "knowing the facts and reaching conclusions of their own which do not flow from their emotions and which are not made for them by others."

But, as we shall see, the comment was misleadingly modest. At a time when inflated fears of the propagandist abounded on every hand, he was trying hard to reassume the protective, neutral coloration of an earlier era. Lee, in fact, was using such apparently prodemocratic language to advance the most conservative of business practices.

His reassuring descriptions of public capacities enabled Lee to take account of mass opinion without capitulating to it. An irrational public would have to be avoided or repressed; a sensible public could be engaged and educated. Most business leaders, he recognized, wanted to believe that their goals could stand up to fair-minded scrutiny.

At the same time, his confidence in conservative business wisdom was deeply felt. Executives were entitled to exercise leadership he said, "by right of character and ability." As a London magazine writer later put the matter, he was "so completely in sympathy with big business that there is no reason to doubt his fundamental sincerity."

Lee would even agree from time to time that public wisdom could expose the error of a client or employer. You can't make good publicity, he would say, out of bad policy. But for the most part, the messages he shaped were designed to modify public opinion and not business practice. To say that the public was reasonable was to say that what was good for the mines and railroads was good for the country.

Lee's outlook reflected his patrician style. He was not asking his clients to love or entertain or even understand the crowd. One gave the public sound information, but there was no need to give it one's heart.

"Courtier to the Crowd" is the label given to Lee in the title of Ray Eldon Hiebert's 1966 biography. But Lee would probably have resisted that description. In his view the "courtiers" were those who appealed to the crowd's heart rather than its head, arousing it against the business sector. When he spoke of public rationality, he was speaking not of "the crowd" but of an ideal public. The public that actually confronted him day by day, he also knew, was a corruptible one. Dealing with such a public required a much more realistic sort of rhetoric:

> The public now rule. We have substituted for the divine right of kings, the divine right of the multitude. The crowd is enthroned. This new sovereign has his courtiers, who flatter and caress precisely as did those who surrounded medieval emperors ... these courtiers are sedulously cultivating the doctrine that to be weak is to be good and that to be strong is to be bad. The demagog is abroad in the land and there are omens that cannot be disregarded.

To "court" the crowd was not only undignified, it was demagogic. It meant catering to its whims and fancies, using gimmicks and low tricks. That was what propagandists did, and nothing worried Lee more than being "tainted as a propagandist."

At one point, even while decrying the abuses of the courtiers, Lee spoke of his admiration for the popular evangelist Billy Sunday. "He speaks the language of the man who rides the trolley car and goes to the ball game, who chews gum and spits tobacco juice," he observed. The passage startled those who would never have expected such a reference from the patrician Ivy Lee. But even in this case, his words were a plea for clarity in making public appeals, not for demagogy.

Unlike other publicists of the day, Lee never talked much about salesmanship. He saw his role, instead, as that of the mediator, the negotiator, the diplomat. He had grown up amid sharp dichotomies, his biographer has theorized—the Old versus the New South, the old versus the new religion. Both personal and social progress meant learning to be "a compromiser, an adjustor, a bridger of worlds." He arranged for the wide distribution in 1922 of a sermon by Harry Emerson Fosdick that pleaded for understanding between fundamentalist and radical theologians. He foresaw the new economic age as one in which "a tendency to play for the whole team would replace the more selfish and introspective personality of the pioneer."

Lee's approach was heightened by his identification with Woodrow Wilson. Both men were Georgian natives, Democrats, the sons of ministers, champion debaters, and Princetonians. Lee emulated Wilson's manner and his outlook. On the other hand, he had little affinity for the publicist president par excellence, Theodore Roosevelt. Lee's style was not so much that of the bully pulpit as of the lawyer's podium.

Not surprisingly, he shared Wilson's view that conflicts, large and small, grew out of secrecy and misunderstanding. He supported Wilson's call for open diplomacy, mourned the American failure to join the League of Nations, worked for the International Committee of the Red Cross, and battled against isolationism. A conservative who hated communism, he nevertheless amazed his associates by supporting diplomatic recognition of the Soviet Union. Stop all maneuvering against the new Russian government and "let in the sunlight," he urged (even in the midst of the anti-Bolshevik hysteria of 1919). This, he said, would be the best way to destroy communism. So strenuously did he argue this case that the conservative Representative Hamilton Fish finally labeled him "a notorious propagandist for Soviet Russia."

Most importantly, Lee believed that better publicity would also dissipate conflict at home. "*Tout comprendre c'est tout pardoner*," he would confidently repeat. "To understand all is to forgive all." The courtiers of the popular press, including the progressive "muckrakers," could be driven back by the bright light of effective publicity. As Lee saw it, muckrakers flourished only because business leaders failed to tell their side of the story.

He wrote an advertisement for Bethlehem Steel in 1916, which insisted (in newspapers across the country):

> We have allowed irresponsible assertions to be made for so long without denial that many people now believe them to be proven facts. We shall make the mistake of silence no longer. Henceforth we shall pursue a policy of publicity. Misinformation will not be permitted to go uncorrected.

From the start, the motto of the Parker and Lee firm had been "Accuracy, Authenticity, and Interest." That strategy had been tested in 1906 when their coal company client, George Baer, in the midst of a massively painful miners' strike, had described himself as one of a small group of capitalists to whom "God in His Infinite Wisdom has given control of the property interests of the country." Talk about an "image problem"!

Lee's response was simply to have the coal industry operators sign a pledge of candor that said, "All our work is done in the open. We aim to supply news." To some extent it worked. Some surprised reporters responded with favorable stories. The same thing happened after Lee talked the Pennsylvania Railroad into releasing complete reports on rail accidents. The grateful company made him a vice president.

In the midst of the bitter Colorado coal strike of 1914, just after the horrors of the Ludlow massacre broke into public view, John D. Rockefeller Jr. called Lee to New York and asked him a perplexing question: "I feel that my father and I are misunderstood. ... I should like to know what your advice would be." Lee told the beleaguered executive to forget about gimmickry or even large-scale advertising. "Absolute frankness" was his recommendation. Rockefeller retained him immediately with the observation, "This is the first advice I have had that does not involve deviousness of one kind or another."

Lee underscored his point when he learned that his client would enter by the back door when he attended a US Senate investigation of the strike. "The days of the rear-door philosophy are over," he announced. Rockefeller Jr. entered by the main aisle, shaking hands with strike leaders as he made his way into the room. Later he would dance with the miners' wives on a Lee-arranged trip to Colorado.

Lee was often credited with suggesting John D. Rockefeller Sr.'s practice of handing out dimes to young children. While it appears that other advisors may have suggested this particular idea, the gradual improvement in the Rockefeller family image owed much to Lee's persistent entreaties.

Lee traveled widely in the last two decades of his life, confident, as Wilson had been, that full and frank publicity could repair the "psychological chasms" on the darkening international front. All would be well if Mussolini and the French would simply level with each other. Stalin ought to be more candid. If only Hitler would be more "open" in his dealings, tensions would be reduced. *Tout comprendre, c'est tout pardonner.*

Lee's rhetorical framing appealed to many idealists, at least for a while. *Editor & Publisher* magazine, a bitter, journalistic enemy of press agentry in all forms, nonetheless credited the Parker and Lee firm as "never sensational, never libelous, always accurate, always trustworthy, always readable." In 1924 the president of the American Association of Newspaper Editors conceded that Lee's publicity was "perfectly legitimate and usually helpful."

Lee's agreeable philosophy reflected age-old hopes for a harmonious, democratic world. And his optimism has also been evident, it must be said, in our own time, witness recent hopeful predictions that the new digital information revolution would dissolve old tensions in a newly "flat" global landscape.

MAKING LIGHT SHINE: THE ROLE OF SENTIMENT

"Let your light so shine before men," was Lee's favorite Bible passage. You do not make your light shine, you just "let" it shine, he would counsel. It was an important distinction. If publicity was not calculated, Lee implied, then it would not be coercive.

The fact of the matter was that many of Lee's premises were faulty. The public, in truth, was not always rational—even when it was properly informed. Nor was rationality always on the side of business. Fundamental conflicts existed between the people and the interests. With words such as those we have already examined, Lee tried earnestly to stare down these unpleasant realities. But when the hard choices were forced on him, he was thoroughly a man of business.

Lee's writings are replete with comments that contradict those we have already cited. "He held within himself the dichotomy of America," is how the Hiebert biography puts it, acknowledging both Lee's Jeffersonian and his Hamiltonian impulses and suggesting that Lee "was unusually able to contain this duality."

From the start, he knew perfectly well that his professional purpose was not merely to "let" but also to "make" his clients' light shine. The publicist had to do more than merely tell the truth, clean the window glass, or raise the curtain.

Lee made the light shine in many ways. An able administrator, he devised large saturation campaigns using movies, newspapers, streetcar posters, leaflets, annual reports, and executive speeches. As early as 1914 he put together long mailing lists of "leaders of opinion" across the country. Later on, he would agree with Walter Lippmann's argument that, in a newly complex world, truth will emerge only if extraordinary efforts were made to uncover, verify, order, and highlight the facts, and then to distribute them broadly.

In 1924 Lee sharpened the argument when he took on President Calvin Coolidge. The president had challenged an audience of newspaper editors to always present "a complete and candid survey of all the facts." The Democratic publicist chose to be outraged. "Will you kindly tell me of any situation in human history which was ever presented to the people in the form of a candid survey of all the facts?" he exclaimed. It is impossible to give all the facts—in support he cited Lippmann—and therefore someone knowledgeable must always make a subjective selection. If partiality (selection) and value (interpretation) turn "fact" into "propaganda," then so be it.

> It is a bad word; I wish I had some substitute for it, but after all it means the effort to propagate ideas and I do not know any real derivative to substitute for the word. All that can be involved in propaganda is a demand, which the public is entitled to make, that when it is given information upon which it is expected to form conclusions, it shall know who is doing the telling, who is responsible for the information.

In this changing context, the once "neutral" publicist could now be compared, said Lee, to a specialized journalist, who sorts and packages the facts and orders them "on the shelves," like a storekeeper. He talked about "marshalling the evidence for his side," even though his handouts were increasingly seen as a screen between his client and the public. More and more the man who had presented himself as a sheet of clear glass was attacked by working journalists as a "buffer."

Lee counterattacked; most of the journalists were in over their heads, he retorted, not an unfamiliar response to unwelcome information in our own time. They are unsophisticated, poorly trained, even lazy; they needed enlightened help to make proper sense of things. To compensate, the modern publicity man was essential.

The problem with Lee's argument, of course, was that even well-motivated publicists could exploit such a vacuum in the service of a particular agenda. He who selects and packages and arranges goods on the shelves (or on a social media feed, one might add) can—even without being devious—say a great deal about what people will purchase. Or what policies they will support. Or whom they will vote for.

Whenever Lee was attacked for undue influence, he responded that he was only telling the truth. Often he was, but many contemporaries felt, as his biographer put it, that Lee could take greater advantage of the press with the truth than most press agents did with fiction.

Improving the mechanics of distributing information was one way in which Lee hedged on the bet he had earlier placed on simple candor. A second telling compromise involved appeals to emotion. Sometimes sentiment could be used to heighten factual appeals. Emotion came to play an increasing role in his advocacy, so much so that one of his critics would come to describe him as a master of "the ancient arts of demagoguery, playing to base emotions and animal instincts." From southern orators, revivalists, and carpetbaggers, Lee was said to have learned to weave the verbal "magic" that "baffled the average man."

Such criticism may unfairly have attributed to Lee some of the skills and sins of his followers. Nonetheless, he had increasingly included the psychology of emotion in his publicity toolbag. "A public to be influenced must feel," he wrote in 1916, citing Wilson's view that "the people are not moved by mind, they are moved by sentiment." Success with crowds could mean organizing their will through the use of symbols. And then the outspoken advocate of public rationality flatly declared, "Crowds do not reason."

The key distinction here was between the "public" and the "crowd." Whenever Lee talked about emotion, he consistently referred to the "crowd" and not to the "public." The crowd craves leadership, and leaders must make the most of "the fundamental currents of human nature." As if debating with himself, he warns his followers not to "exaggerate the influence of reason in determining the acts of mankind at large." Leaders must appeal to "these same elementary crowd impulses." Yet in virtually the same breath, Lee can be found saying that the glass of publicity "should not color; it should not distort."

This fundamental tension was evident throughout Lee's career. Writing just before his death in a treatise candidly called *International Propaganda*, he suggested that exploiting emotion could help move nations closer together. And yet, he adds (in a comment which seems to have been a secondary thought), "there comes a time when it is necessary to appeal to reason." Like so many others, then and now, he very much wanted to have it both ways.

WRESTLING WITH INCONSISTENCIES

When Ivy Lee argued strongly for the power of unvarnished truth, he may simply have been overcompensating for a plea he knew was dubious. But it seems more likely that his inconsistency was a genuine consequence of his personal history and temperament. He worked hard to grapple with the contradictions.

Late in his life, he would share an interesting approach, quoting from Goethe's Faust.

> When you are in earnest, do you need a search for words?
>
> If from the soul the language does not come
>
> By its own impulse
>
> In vain you strive.
>
> Never hope to stir the hearts of men
>
> And mould the souls of many into one
>
> By words which come not native from the heart.

What Goethe and Lee seem to suggest here is that the key to molding minds is sincerity. It is subjective and not objective accuracy that is essential. If someone is "in earnest," that person will be persuasive. What seems to count most is not that the leader has made a rational argument but that one's words must come "native from the heart." It seems to be a relatively permissive standard.

A decade earlier, shortly after the First World War, Lee had offered this thought. "Even the most clever man, if he constantly either lies, or half lies, or takes an unsocial position, sooner or later will be found out by the public." This fallback position transfers the responsibility from the messenger to the audience. If errors are passed along, well, the public will catch them in the final audit. If the public does not catch them, then in Lee's system, perhaps they were not errors at all.

In other writings Lee insisted that all one could ask of public information in the end was that every communication be signed by the person responsible for it so that the public could hold someone accountable. The test here was not even a publicist's sincerity but his nerve.

By assigning the responsibility for results to a self-validating theory, Lee was freer to be an absolute loyalist for his clients. The courtroom analogy helped Lee resolve the contradictions in his rhetoric: the lawyer was both counsel to his client and an officer of the court. Because a presumably rational public jury would hear his case, he could serve the whole by representing the part. One of his first articles, published in 1904, even claimed that "the lawyer does not inquire into the motives—be they sinister or benevolent—of his clients."

As the years went by, Lee's image as a shrewd huckster and manager of news grew to extreme and unfair proportions. He was, after all, the most prominent pioneer in a field that was quickly becoming a prodigious public villain. Upton Sinclair in *The Brass Check* in 1919 popularized an unshakeable nickname, "Poison Ivy." Carl Sandburg somewhat hyperbolically wrote in the *New York Call* in 1915 that Lee was "a paid liar, a cunning, slimy charlatan, below the level of the hired gunman and slugger." In *The 42nd Parallel*, John Dos Passos created an unpleasant, amoral publicity man named J. Ward Morehouse, modeled, he said, on Lee. In 1925 the magazine that had praised him so lavishly in 1910, *Editor & Publisher*, described his work as "a blatant fraud" and "an outrage."

What was happening, too, was that the public was losing confidence in its own capacities and finding villains to blame. A hero for many in the balmy days of "pitiless publicity" before the war, Lee became a symbol of all that people feared when they spoke of propaganda in a later and more nervous era. Felix Frankfurter summed it up in a letter to President Franklin D. Roosevelt in 1934:

> I venture to say, however, that particularly in these restless days in which foolishness and fanaticism and self-interest are exploited by professional poisoners of the public mind, by the Ivy Lees and the Bernays, it becomes even more important than it was in the days of T.R. and Woodrow Wilson for the President to do what you are able to do with such extraordinary effectiveness; namely, to give guidance to the public in order to rally them to the general national interest.

Even as Frankfurter attacked "professional poisoners of the public mind," he saw the antidote in an opinion molder he trusted. This simultaneous rejection and embrace of the instruments of propaganda was typical of many engaged leaders of the era. Twenty years earlier, Senator Robert La Follette faced off against Lee in a battle concerning a railroad rate increase. Calling Lee's defensive publicity project "a monument of shame," the Wisconsin senator entered all of Lee's campaign materials into the *Congressional Record*, causing Lee to note sardonically that La Follette had run up a government printing bill as large as the railroads' expenses for the original campaign itself.

Meanwhile, La Follette, having worked himself into a characteristic moral frenzy, introduced a bill that would have outlawed any effort to influence the government regulators by writing letters, articles, or any other forms of communication. It was a bizarre proposal to come from the outspoken civil libertarian whose political motto was "The Truth Shall Make You Free." But then, that was frequently Lee's motto as well.

Clearly, now as then, it takes a strong sense of restraint to honor in all circumstances the idea of a free marketplace of ideas, open to views with which one may vigorously disagree.

If the challenge was occasionally too much for Robert La Follette, then perhaps we should not be too surprised at the lapses of Ivy Lee.

Perhaps the central episode in establishing Lee's manipulative image was the Colorado coal strike of 1914. Lee edited a series of bulletins released from Colorado that turned out to be one-sided at best and in some cases blatantly false. The bulletins provoked a national controversy, and while Lee was not responsible for the factual errors, he was blamed for them. (Among the first and loudest to rake this new muck, damning those who were "poisoning public opinion," was a young journalist by the name of George Creel—a subject of the next chapter.)

Outright untruths were rare, however. What bothered observers more were the half-truths, the selectivity, the screening, and the fact that Lee's idealistic protestations seemed so disingenuous. One story that made the rounds told of a speech Lee wrote for Bethlehem Steel magnate Charles Schwab. It opened by describing three speech texts that Schwab had at hand, one written "by my friend here" (pointing to Ivy Lee). Schwab announced that he was "going to throw them all away and speak to you from the heart." Whereupon Schwab smiled at the applause and, speaking "from the heart," make the speech that Lee had written.

Many observers felt that their worries about Lee were confirmed in 1934 when his worst misstep was revealed. He had worked in the 1920s for an American subsidiary of the German dye trust, I.G. Farben, and later had advised both the parent company and the Nazi government on how to improve their American image. Their treatment of the Jews was just "foreign to the American mentality" he told them. He also suggested that Hitler's storm troops should be explained away as anti-Communist civil forces. Lee broke sharply with the Nazis as their terrorism increased and was never paid in full for his services.

In the spring of 1934, however, a congressional committee headed by John W. McCormack of Massachusetts (a later Speaker of the House) investigated the entire matter. The committee seemed satisfied with Lee's explanations and focused greater interest on another US public relations firm more deeply involved with the Germans, headed by Carl Byoir. But in July, just ten days after stories of Hitler's "blood purge" had set off a wave of global revulsion, the House Un-American Activities Committee released the news of its secret hearings and of Lee's earlier German involvements. His reputation collapsed. The publicist retreated into silence. Four months later he died.

The presence of intellectual inconsistencies in his thinking would probably have seemed an academic matter for Lee. If the policies he was promoting were correct, if he was working sincerely in the general interest, then argumentative logic, mechanical proficiency, and emotional appeals all worked to the same practical end. "Accuracy, Authenticity, Interest"— so abideth these three, and to busy practitioners, what did it really matter which was the greatest?

Throughout much of his career, social and selfish interest coincided for Ivy Lee. What was effective overlapped for him with what was true. He did not have to feel that he was bamboozling the public. But as time passed, the profession that Ivy Lee helped found would be tainted by the instability of these compromises. And never was their insufficiency so apparent as when Ivy Lee chatted cheerfully in the summer of 1933 with Adolf Hitler and Joseph Goebbels, advising his hosts to be more candid in explaining their policies.

Lee was talking with men who were convinced that reason had little to do with either fame or power and that fear and falsehood could produce conviction. Ivy Lee had sold publicity to himself and to his country as a tool of social harmony, but in a dissonant world, actual practice would often contradict his happy theory. When Lee talked publicity with Hitler and Goebbels, he was dealing with men who had already moved a great deal further along a road that he, like many of his countrymen, had only begun to walk.

CHAPTER 5

The Propagandist as Progressive Warrior

N o one embraced the potential of a new information age more enthusias-
tically or wielded the skills of "publicity" more effectively than Theodore
Roosevelt. Motivated by a deep fear of the uncontrolled mob and by his own
"persistent desire to impose himself on others" (as the historian Richard Hof-
stadter has put it), he did not even pretend to worship slavishly the opinions of
a democratic public. "Let me have free access to the channels of publicity," he
said, "and I care not who makes my country's laws." Later he wrote, "I simply
made up my mind what they [the public] ought to think, and then I did my best
to get them to think it." He was the first president to create a press area for
journalists at the White House, the first to appoint a press secretary, the first
to hold regular press conferences, and the first to campaign personally on a
wide national scale, even as a vice presidential candidate in 1900. He described
his presidency as the "Bully Pulpit," and he worked hand in glove with Progressive journalists—famously known as the "muckrakers"—to advance his reform
agenda. (The term was actually Roosevelt's invention. Intended to describe
some of his critics, it boomeranged and came to describe his allies as well.)

Other Progressive leaders joined Roosevelt in an enthusiastic embrace of "publicity." Wisconsin senator Robert La Follette launched his own magazine in 1909
to "rally and rouse the people." Senator Hiram Johnson of California argued in 1910
that "a publicity bureau" was a sine qua non of political achievement. In 1912 former
Hollywood mayor George A. Dunlop launched a publicly owned newspaper, the
Los Angeles Municipal News, to advance the same objectives.

In that same year, a longtime muckraker named George Kibbe Turner took to
the pages of *McClure's Magazine*, the lead muckraking outlet, where his had long
been a familiar voice. *McClure's* had earlier attacked big business for "Manufacturing Public Opinion" to support reactionary views, but Turner used the same title, in
the same magazine, to celebrate publicity's positive potential. His subtitle heralded
"The New Art of Making Presidents by Press Bureau"—citing the 1912 campaigns of
Roosevelt and La Follette as examples. The machine manufacture of public opinion

was not only the frightening tool of entrenched privilege but the liberating instrument of the zealous reformer.

ENTER GEORGE CREEL

Turner's salute to the machinery of publicity did not mention a fellow muckraker who was soon to build the greatest publicity machine the nation (and the world) had yet seen. Constructed almost overnight, it would quickly rally an uncertain country in support for the First World War while also serving as the "great training school" for the advertising and public relations industries of the postwar years.

The man who built and defended that machinery shared well-established Progressive attitudes toward public information—exuberant, disarming, conflicted, naive. And his postwar efforts both to amplify and to justify the impact of his work have been echoed by all manner of propagandists ever since.

His career helped create the concept of the propaganda warrior. For decades afterward the very mention of the new "P" word could still bring the response "Oh, yes. What was that fellow's name, the one with the Belgian babies with their hands cut off and all of that? Yes, that's it. George Creel!"

George Creel had nothing to do with the stories of the Belgian babies and very little to do with the other atrocity stories since linked to the propaganda legend. But his name did indeed become a household word throughout the war and its aftermath. For in 1917 and 1918—on millions upon millions of pamphlets, flyers, advertisements, posters, billboards, and even the slides thrown nightly onto the screens of five thousand neighborhood theaters—the legend appeared: "The Committee on Public Information, George Creel, Chairman."

***

Born in rural Missouri in 1876, Creel was educated in Kansas City and started a weekly newspaper there, the *Independent*, in 1899. He became an impassioned crusader, attacking the local Prendergast political machine, advocating a rehabilitation farm for prostitutes, and generally promoting his publication as "A Clean Paper for Clean People." He also allied himself with a local club called the University Militant, designed as "a new intellectual and spiritual establishment ... free of control by both money and the mob." Its founder, Charles Ferguson, made Creel the group's "director of propaganda" at a time when that word had new connotations that were exciting but not yet malign.

In 1908 Creel published his first book, a collection of impassioned poetry called *Quatrains of Christ*. These lines are typical:

> O let me take the world's old worn-out tongue
>
> And crush it to the vague from which it sprung,

Then fashion from the inarticulate,

New songs to vary those that have been sung.

The poet Edwin Markham described Creel's volume as "one of the four or five best books of verse among the many that have come to me from the younger American writers." The book's preface by Julian Hawthorne tellingly described Creel's communication style:

> There is no evasion or compromise in his speech. ... His belief and tes-
> timony are as naif as that of a little child ... there is little concern with
> arguments; he appeals to the interior witness of the adoring heart ...
> he has felt the truth himself, deep in his soul, and he cannot do oth-
> erwise than give it forth with all his soul and strength.

Creel went on to serve as a vitriolic editor of the *Rocky Mountain News* in Denver from 1911 to 1913. His article on the Colorado coal strike in *Harper's* in 1914 helped turn the nation's attention to the publicity activities of the Rockefeller interests and, eventually, to the work of Ivy Lee.

But journalism alone—even at its muckraking best—would not be enough to reform the nation, Creel soon concluded. As his reputation grew, he recommended that the new president, Woodrow Wilson, set up "some machinery ... for the proper presentation of facts," in order to counter the "overwhelming advantage" of pro-business publicity.

Creel's self-righteous zeal could sometimes alarm even fellow Progressives. When he charged in 1915 that another reform-minded editor had been corrupted by Rockefeller money, the *New Republic* was outraged. Creel, the magazine concluded, is a "reckless and incompetent person ... determined to make a noise no matter what canon of truthfulness he violates." Creel replied in kind, justifying his work as an "agitator" because he was always fighting for the underdog. The *New Republic* editors, on the other hand, progressive as they might be, represented what he saw as an elitist tribe. "The antagonism between us," he warned, is "as instinctive and inevitable as that of the house cat for the street dog."

Through all his years of combat, Creel had admired one particular hero. Ever since he heard Woodrow Wilson speak at a Kansas City high school in 1905, he had been promoting him for president. He campaigned for Wilson in 1911 and 1912 and published an enthusiastic campaign book, *Wilson and the Issues*, in 1916. Wilson's opponents, said Creel, were keeping the public "so busy feeling, that they will not have time for thinking." This "stammer" would be overcome only by the countervailing voice of a leader like Wilson, who could articulate "the ancient faith" and realize again "the oneness of the American people."

When America entered the war in April 1917, Creel wrote a vigorous letter of concern to the president. As he later recalled:

> I explained to him that the need was for expression not repression,
> and urged a campaign that would carry our war aims and peace terms

not only to the United States, but to every neutral country, and also in England, France, and Italy. ... He sent for me and after approving my proposal, drafted me to act as active chairman. No other person was considered for the place.

So it was that "Mr. Creel woke up one morning to find himself the American Northcliffe," as one observer put it, referring to the press-lord who dominated Britain's wartime publicity machinery. Freshly appointed, Creel then set out one bright spring day, in the company of a young War Department officer named Douglas MacArthur, to locate an office and set up shop.

Some shop. Its bureaus proliferated weekly. "Looking back, it seems a miracle," said Creel, that the Committee on Public Information (CPI) survived "the terrific strain of creation."

The improvisational atmosphere added to a spirit of adventure and rapport. We were all idealists and "full of beans" one recruit, Hamilton Owens, would later remember. He recalled his colleagues "as amateurs, mostly, novelists, professors, a few beatniks, only two experienced newsmen and a dozen or so pretty girls who wanted to do their bit for democracy." Creel would write afterward of the "gangling, youngish" and "rosy-cheeked" idealists who were forever bursting into his office to announce some new idea for winning "the fight for the mind of mankind."

Creel's committee members were Secretary of the Navy Josephus Daniels, Secretary of War Newton Baker, and Secretary of State Robert Lansing. Lansing preferred old-fashioned censorship and distrusted Creel personally. Baker was indifferent and preoccupied with military matters. Daniels, a former journalist, was the only member of the committee to participate actively in its work.

Additionally, Creel's independent access to the White House rendered meaningless the concept of committee planning. Wilson sensed in Creel a kindred spirit and gave him extraordinary prerogatives. It was said that Wilson ran the war through three men, Newton Baker, Bernard Baruch, and George Creel—a sudden elevation both for Creel and for the role of information in wartime.

FOREIGN MODELS: AMERICAN CAUTIONS

As early as September 1914, one month after the war began, a *New York Times* editorial observed that "this is the first press agent's war." But initially it was foreign press agents who were in the spotlight. Britain and Germany worked vigorously to win over the American public, focusing mostly on discrediting the pernicious publicity efforts of their enemies.

As it happened, the Germans' activities were easily exposed and, once exposed, seemed more sinister. The most important example was the German's loss on July 24, 1915, of the Albert portfolio, a collection of documents describing their stunningly ambitious US publicity plans. (Amazingly, the portfolio was snatched by a federal agent from a New York elevated railway car when its owner left it behind.) The negative public reaction when these objectives were exposed was damaging, to say the least. One German propagandist, George Sylvester Viereck, later compared the loss of the Albert portfolio to Germany's decisive military loss in the Battle of the Marne.

Some postwar analyses credited German propaganda with delaying American entry into the war from 1914 to early 1917. But most commentators, including some from Germany, concluded that those efforts had been badly bungled and had often backfired.

British efforts, on the other hand, were more subtle, emphasizing quiet personal contacts and extensive letter writing by their Canadian-born agent Gilbert Parker. What hurt the British cause, ironically, was their effort to perpetrate atrocity stories about German soldiers in the first months of the war. While some of the frightening tales were later validated, many Americans treated the horror stories as evidence of British perfidy rather than German barbarism. The esteemed writer Upton Sinclair typified this reaction when he wrote in 1927, "I am one of the hundred and ten million suckers who swallowed the hook of the British official propaganda, conducted by an eminent bourgeois novelist, Gilbert Parker, who afterward was knighted for what he did to me."

Some regretful British participants also confessed to some of the "lying" they themselves had done. A considered view, however, is that it was neither American gullibility nor British publicity skills that led the United States into the war. It can be argued, in fact, that the power of wartime propaganda was largely itself a myth, created by both sides as they exaggerated the work of their opponents. Then as now, attributing fake news to one's adversaries was a highly tempting strategy.

When George Creel came to his post, he was determined that the word *propaganda*, even though he had used it proudly a decade earlier, should not be applied to American publicity. By this time, propaganda was what the other side did. Creel would go to enormous lengths, therefore, to preserve the committee's credibility, and he would go to even greater lengths to advertise the fact that this was exactly what he was doing.

MOBILIZING AMERICA'S TALENT

A muckraking rival and frequent Creel critic, Mark Sullivan, while commending some of Creel's own work, also emphasized the talent of Creel's team. In *Our Times*, his highly influential six-volume history of America from 1900 to 1925, he described how "Creel mobilized—but let us cease detail—and merely say Creel assembled leaders of about every group in America whose occupation or function was in the field of imagination, creative art, or publicity."

Creel agreed. "It still amazes me how few mistakes I made in the selection of men," he wrote to one of those men, Edward Bernays, in 1941. Many had come from journalism, a veritable "roll call of the muckrakers." Others came from advertising. "Today every great advertising man in the United States is working for the Committee on Public Information," he declared in 1918. In turn, the war spurred the development of the postwar advertising industry. "The war taught us the power of propaganda," said one of the country's leading postwar entrepreneurs, Roger Babson. "Now when we have anything to sell to the American people, we know how to sell it."

Creel's team also drew heavily on the country's colleges and universities. At the head of the parade was Guy Stanton Ford, a history professor and later president of the University of Minnesota. He supervised Creel's writing corps and chaired the Division of Civic and Educational Cooperation. An impressive array of academicians followed his lead, conducting what Ford called "a war Chautauqua."

The prominence of academics in the war effort, ironically, would later contribute to a powerful antipropaganda backlash. Many participating intellectuals would later feel embarrassed by their CPI service. As one embittered critic put it, they had sacrificed their "intellectual gifts upon the altar of the nation."

The propaganda experience also helped reinforce the current of anti-intellectualism in American life. Gustave Le Bon, as we have seen, was ready to trust the wisdom of forty water carriers over forty academicians. *The Nation*'s proudly liberal editor, Oswald Garrison Villard, similarly wrote that he would rather trust "five hundred Americans of the farms and villages than a similar number of ... college graduates." George Sylvester Viereck proactively suggested that the academic mind was particularly vulnerable to mass persuasion because of its tendency to accept too many premises. Others speculated (perhaps with some cause!) that intellectuals are more vulnerable because they are required to have opinions on too many topics.

Whatever their later culpability, thousands of America's best writers and scholars joined the 150,000 employed and volunteer CPI workers in 1917. Their output of books and pamphlets alone exceeded seventy-five million. Perhaps their most remarkable feat involved the famous Four Minute Men, some 75,000 volunteers who delivered four-minute patriotic speeches in 5,200 community theaters and meeting halls across the country each evening, normally in "the first intermission after eight o'clock." By war's end, the number of such speeches had reached more than 750,000. "Broadcasting before radio," historians called it. Or, as we might now say, social media before the internet.

The CPI also put out a daily government newspaper, *The Official Bulletin*. Other divisions produced films, posters, ads, cartoons, articles, and photographs. Special agencies looked after labor and industrial relations, press relations, the foreign born, women, wireless information, undersea cables, and other overseas connections. And the net cost of all this was only about $5 million.

What did it all add up to? For Creel it was clear. "There is not a corner of the earth today that does not know us as we are ... and knowing us they like us and trust us. From being the most misunderstood nation in the world, America became the most popular." In enemy countries, "the publicity offensive" sapped resistance and shortened the fighting, he submitted in 1919. At home, the CPI's impact, according to a landmark history called *Words That Won the War*, was "a burning eagerness to believe, to conform."

That comprehensive 1939 book, written by James R. Mock and Cedric Larson, described the domestic impact vividly:

> Consider the case of one Midwestern family. They lived on a quarter section of farmland a dozen miles from the railroad, telegraph, and post office. The nearest daily newspaper was published at the far end of the next county, seventy-five miles away. No through road passed near their farm, they had seen pavement only a few times in their lives, and they had no phone. Normally they paid scant attention to public affairs. Their only aim in life, so it seemed, was to bring in the golden harvest. Yet when this simple, uneducated family, sat down to a thresher's supper in the summer of 1918, they were more conscious of the World War than many more literate people had been of any war since fighting began.

> The information they received was precisely the same kind that millions of their fellow citizens were getting at the same moment. It came through the county weekly, the daily papers picked up now and then in the general store, the movies at the county seat, the state fair in September, the verses the children learned at the township school and the colored maps they brought home with them, the posters on telephone poles, the pre-fabricated prayers of the preacher on Sunday, pamphlets in the pews, patriotic buttons, window stickers, and, yes, through rumors as well.

For some, the potential was inspiring. One CPI employee marveled at how such machinery might possibly even convert revolutionary Russia to "the support of democracy and humanity." But others were less sanguine. Speaking for many on the left, *The Nation* reminded its readers that what the government had actually discovered was "new and hitherto undreamed-of ways of fortifying their control over the masses of people."

ENEMIES AND EMOTIONS

When Creel took his post, Mark Sullivan asked how Wilson could make a censor out of "the most aggressive and daring of newspaper men, the most insistent on pitiless publicity, the most violent of the muckrakers?" The answer of course was that Creel was hired not as a censor but as a crusader. He was, as Sullivan later wrote, "fervidly temperamental in a way that pleased and amused." He was "pungent, racy, robust." On a platform, Creel became "a raging reformer," compounding "the more berserker qualities of Danton, Marat, and Charlotte Corday."

Other recollections supported Sullivan's assessment. Once, when successfully defending himself in court against a libel suit, Creel had refused to withdraw his claim that a certain "enemy of the people" was fit to be hanged. Surely he meant that figuratively, his own lawyer had assured the jury. Whereupon Creel is reported to have shouted across the courtroom, "No, I meant it. The hemp! The hemp!"

Sullivan's comparison of Creel to the French revolutionaries accorded with Creel's self-image. One of his heroes was Thomas Paine, whose example persuaded him that ardent pamphleteering could create public opinion. When the popular publication *Everybody's Magazine* announced a postwar series in which Creel would tell about his work, it added this observation: "Creel is a man who always attracts bitter enemies and wins ardent support. But in the gigantic [wartime] task ... his enemies far exceeded his friends."

Foremost among those enemies were Republican members of Congress. Throughout his tenure, they probed and harassed him and finally cut his funds, creating havoc with the CPI's shutdown procedures. "Uncle Joe" Cannon, a Republican House leader for forty-six years, suggested that Creel "ought to be taken by the nape of his neck and slack of his pants and thrown into space." Anti-Wilson senators like Henry Cabot Lodge repeatedly called for his resignation. Another, Lawrence Sherman, described him as "a violent rakehell of depraved journalism." Even a Democratic senator, James Reed, called him a "licensed liar."

Creel said that every such attack "has seen me die a thousand deaths," but he did little to repair relations. He was suited to the role of lightning rod, and he relished replying in kind. He could not speak about Congress, he said in 1917, because "he had not been slumming in years." As the comment made its way across the country, he offered his resignation to Wilson, but the president refused it.

He regarded the fund cutoff as a "treasonous" act, noting how its congressional proponents had gone unpunished even though "they shot a soldier for a passive act like sleeping at his post." He was particularly bitter about Lodge, whose mind, he recalled, was like the New England soil, highly cultivated but naturally sterile. "An exceedingly dull man and a very vain one—deadly combination—his vanity fosters his ignorance by persistent refusal to confess it." He summed up the matter this way:

> Let me make the statement therefore, calmly and carefully, that domestic disloyalty, the hostility of neutrals, and the lies of German propagandists, all combined, were not half so hard to combat as the persistent malignance of a partisan group in the Congress of the United States.

There was no point in even trying to establish good relations with Congress, he said, continuing his "calm" and "careful" analysis: "One might as well have talked about establishing 'closer relations' with a water-moccasin."

DEFENDING THE RECORD: TRUTH, CANDOR, AND REASON

As much as he disdained his critics, Creel worked hard to respond to their criticisms, especially in a number of energetic postwar books and articles. Even as he lauded the success of wartime propaganda, he was at pains to convince his fellow citizens of its public legitimacy. Over time, he found three convenient ways to explain himself.

His first and most important defense was that the CPI had told the truth. Only four serious charges of deception were leveled at the CPI, he contended again and again, and he painstakingly responded to each of them.

His enemies, for instance, had made political capital out of the so-called Fourth of July Fake, an enthusiastic Creel report of victory in a submarine battle. Creel was able to verify his account with a report from the commanding officer, and he gave an entire chapter to his clarification in his postwar book *How We Advertised America*. An additional "Three Aircraft Lies" had also been held against him; he persuasively explained away each of them.

The striking point in all of this was Creel's claim that he had resolved all doubts about his practices by answering those petty charges. "Consider for moment!!" he begs his readers:

> More than six thousand separate and distinct news releases, each one dealing with an importance; some half-hundred and distinct pamphlets, brimmed with detail; seventy-five thousand Four Minute Men speaking nightly; other hundreds delivering more extended addresses regularly; thousands of advertisements; countless motion and still pictures, posters and painted signs; war expositions; intimate contacts with foreign language groups; the Official Bulletin appearing daily for two years; and in every capital of the world, outside the Central Powers, offices and representatives, served by daily cable and mail services rich in possibilities for mistake. All done by an organization forced to function from the moment of its creation, working at all times under extremist pressure, handicapped by insufficient funds and harassed by partisanship. And only the four charges! The record stands unparalleled for honesty, accuracy and high purpose.

But what of it? In fact, the four stories were the least of his critic's worries. Nor were those stories responsible for the guilt complexes of so many Creel employees, who confessed with Will Irwin: "We never told the whole truth—not by any manner of means." Surely those who worried about subtle appeals and slants and selections and innuendos received little satisfaction from Creel's overly literal response.

Still, Creel's defense was not entirely irrelevant. He had determined from the start that he would avoid the errors and exaggerations that had backfired on the Europeans. Moreover, as Irwin would later write, there was really "no need of lying." Preaching, yes, and preaching a one-sided case, maybe, but deliberate distortions, never.

In describing it all later on, Creel could not resist overstatement: "No nation ever made a clearer or more truthful presentation of its case, not only to our own people, but to the world." He was proud of his record, with some justification in the opinion of many, including David M. Kennedy, in his much-heralded 1980 history of America at war. Given that record, Creel was determined not to be punished for a sin he had worked so hard to avoid.

Creel's second line of defense was that the information he provided was full and complete, at least insofar as military security permitted. Just as he did not put out lies, neither did he commit what Irwin called "lies of suppression." After all, some of the central struggles of his career had been against government secrecy. His mantra for the committee was simple: "We do not touch censorship at any point." While he did possess certain prohibitive powers, he found even minimal censorship tasks so repulsive that, at the end of his two long years, "I fell to my knees and offered up a fervent prayer that just as I had been America's first official censor so I would live in history as the last."

Creel believed, religiously, in the power of expression. It was the reason he took the job. He sounded no theme louder than the contrast between publicity and secrecy. He believed in Progressive values as Ivy Lee believed in business wisdom, and for both, the new powers of publicity meant that people the world over would soon be able to share their particular happy visions.

In short, Creel would say, it was what people knew—not what they could be kept from knowing—that would shape their behavior. The task was not to keep the people in the dark, but to stir them to buy Liberty Bonds and to send their sons to die in muddy trenches. In theory at least, that required "unparalleled openness." The public should see "every blade of grass growing in wartime Washington." If any press censorship might be needed, then it would be voluntary. Yes, voluntary censorship.

Creel did issue press "guidelines," however, and as time went along they often had a compulsory effect. He would always describe his consultations with the press as a form of persuasion, but people were now beginning to learn the great new lesson of the propaganda age: skillful, all-dominating persuasion can also be a form of compulsion.

Creel's third line of defense was that he had avoided emotionalism and prioritized rational arguments. It was a less plausible argument than his claims about accuracy and openness. In a 1918 article, he forcefully insisted that his single goal had been to set down the issues in black and white, "to put things so simply that even a child could grasp just what we meant by democracy." Public opinion, he argued, "has its base in reason, … rather than any temporary excitement or any passing passion of the moment. We have never approached any emotion of hate. We have never made an appeal to the emotions."

That was patently untrue. It did not square with Creel's later statement about welding "a white hot mass instinct," nor did it square with a good part of the committee's work. Yes, he rejected the worst of the atrocity stories, telling the British quite abruptly that they would have to peddle their own lies. But he also appropriated some of them, as the historian Arthur

Link concluded. The Creel Committee also did its share in implanting a deep American hatred of the Kaiser and of many things German.

Yet, in the eyes of most historians, Creel's work is now seen as relatively restrained. The excesses of many militant voices, public and private, went well beyond those of the CPI, but the committee was better known. In a sense, it was too successful. To its name and to Creel's were thus attributed the worst sins of other propagandists. Creel was a convenient whipping boy, the great historian of American journalism, Frank Luther Mott, has said, but he did not deserve to be one.

Sensing that danger, Creel actually went on the attack against emotional extremists, ridiculing, thundering, and (finally) antagonizing an intensely patriotic segment of the American population. He also conscientiously defended the much-maligned foreign born, including German Americans. He denounced "the certain savage something that thrills to the Man Hunt," disowning "intolerances and bigotries," "noise," and "hysteria." "The government," he declared, "is not responsible for mobs that hang innocent men, that paint houses yellow, and that run up and down the country trying to crush honest discussion. ... I can conceive of no greater tragedy than that, out of stupid rages, out of the elevation of the mob spirit above reason, discussion should be stifled."

From the other side, perhaps predictably, came charges that Creel was too mild, too bloodless. The National Security League and the American Defense Society complained constantly. Creel's restraint, they said, actually gave "aid and comfort to the enemy," when it should be telling Americans "why they should hate the enemy they are expected to meet and kill." Frank Cobb, the editor of the *New York World*, was one of several journalists who saw "weakness" in Creel's approach.

In three ways then, by stressing the accuracy, the fullness, and the supposed rationality of his communications, Creel tried to stave off the critical attacks. Overall, the reality was probably closer to Creel's own assessment than many have thought. But even if Creel's three claims were valid, important questions still remain. What, above all, do his responses say about the issue of control versus consent that so worried defenders of democracy? In practice, George Creel rightly felt that his record on these matters was more reassuring than many realized. But it was his own exultant rhetoric that had helped arouse a deep sense of public trepidation.

RELIGIOUS PASSION AND MILITARY ZEAL

Like other exemplary propagandists then and since, George Creel could be as unconstrained in flattery as in calumny. His book about Wilson in 1920 allowed for no blemish, acknowledged no error. Wilson was not merely a great speaker: "As long as the world lasts his addresses of singular power and beauty will stand as the ultimate exposition of human faith in the practicability of liberty, justice, and fraternity." It was as if, by overreaching himself linguistically, Creel could create the simple realities his emotions demanded. He was not a man of limits or restraints, as Sullivan indicated in his 1917 critique, but rather of an almost "primitive violence." "The President might just as appropriately have appointed Billy Sunday. ... What Sunday is to religion, Creel is to politics ... a crusader, a bearer of the fiery cross."

Creel's style was often discussed in religious parlance. His *Quatrains of Christ* in 1908 had expressed his yearning to make "the world's worn-out tongue" sing "new songs" and to feel "the great kaleidoscopic surge of men." Like his propagandist heirs, he was uncomfortable amid qualifications, subtleties, and procedural norms and niceties. In his heart he knew that he was right, and he thus could work to mold public opinion without worrying about public will. Intellectual humility and a sense of balance were not the virtues of passionate preachers.

Creel saw the First World War as "a holy war," and American soldiers were "Pershing's Crusaders." Wilson himself was the "messiah." As Creel saw it, "The world hopeless despairing, turned to us as the forlorn of Galilee turned to Christ, not knowing, but believing, not asking, but trusting."

On the title page of *How We Advertised America* in 1920, he recalled his work as carrying "the Gospel of Americanism to Every Corner of the Globe." The CPI practiced "propaganda in the true sense of the word, meaning the propagation of the faith." And again: "Never once throughout the war did I have a doubt as to the wisdom and justice of our propaganda, preaching the Fourteen Points in particular with gospel fervor." One of his Four Minute Men, E.L Saintsbury, recalled that his own theater speeches were similar to the "clang and fervor" of a revival meeting when it came under Billy Sunday's spell.

Creel believed, above all, in the potential of words to organize a fragmented society. Presidential leadership was the only answer to the "public stammer" created by those who "manufacture hysteria."

As time passed, Creel began to acknowledge more explicitly the coercive dimensions of his work. The metaphors that came more naturally now were military ones. He anticipated quite directly later commentary about the "weaponization of information." His work at the CPI had been "as hard a battle as any fought in France." Each effort to destroy the German lies was like an attack on "a machine gun nest." The CPI's words were "the shrapnel," but his job was "to determine the cost-effective way to fire it." Each act of communication had to be "aimed as a rifle is aimed and driving to its mark with the precision of a bullet." Wilson's speeches, of course, were "our most effective weapon."

In his 1920 book, Creel cited this poem by Wallace Irwin, extending the military metaphor:

> But now as I study that row upon row / Of wind-blown engravings I feel satisfaction
>
> Deep down in my star-spangled heart, for I know / How Art put on khaki and went into action.

Creel's introduction to the book made the same point.

> Back of the firing line, back of armies and navies, back of the great
> supply depots, another struggle waged with the same intensity, and
> with almost equal significance attaching to its victories and defeats. It
> was the fight for the minds of men, for the "conquest of their convic-
> tions," and the battle-line ran through every home in every country.

Creel's goal had been not only a "mere surface unity, but a passionate belief ... that should weld the people of the United States into one white-hot mass instinct." The argument belied, as we have seen, the ardently rationalistic claims he had made earlier. What had to be driven home, he now said, was that "all business was the nation's business, and every task a common task for a single purpose."

Creel's idealist plea for the League of Nations, entitled *The War, the World and Wilson* (1920), continued in this vein. He argued, more than a year after the Armistice, that the coun- ✗ try's "first task is to get back to a war footing as far as the national morale is concerned." Yes, that could involve a kind of coercion, he acknowledged, but since the values for which he worked were "liberal," he insisted that the people were merely being "coerced to be free." The phrase seemed similar in import to his claims about censorship being voluntary. And what of those who refused to go along with the leadership's coercive messages? Well, once again, they were simply "enemies of the people."

Moral leadership required a hero who could dominate "undeveloped minds" and "in large measure control conduct." Yes, in time, Creel would also acknowledge that some words might have an evil effect, causing "a certain suspension of the mental processes." When that happened, he even admitted, demagogues could replace heroes.

In 1923, as the futility of the recent war became more evident, and especially as the promises of Wilson's postwar objectives collapsed, Creel even joined those who blamed the outcome on bad propagandists, especially in the immediate aftermath of the fighting. They had "killed public opinion, or rather deafened it, confused it, bored it, disgusted it," so that "even existence of a forceful, effective public opinion is much to be doubted." In a series of magazine articles written under the name of "Uncle Henry," Creel reflected sadly on the collapse of his global dream. He (and Uncle Henry) wanted to "work out some plan for makin' good report as interstin' as evil report," but that would take "well ... maybe a genius like Edison."

Wilson, not surprisingly, had seen it all coming, as Creel told it. The president had been standing with him on the deck of the *George Washington* in 1919, headed for the ill-fated peace talks in Paris, with evening coming on, "his face as black as the grey stretch of sunless water." "It is a great thing you have done," the president told the chair of the CPI:

> But I am wondering if you have not unconsciously spun a net for me
> from which there is no escape. It is to America that the whole world

turns today, not only with its wrongs, but with its hopes and grievances. The hungry expect us to feed them, the roofless look to us for shelter, the sick of heart and body depend upon us for cure. All of these expectations have in them the quality of terrible urgency. There must be no delay. It has been so always. People will endure their tyrants for years, but they tear their deliverers to pieces if a millennium is not created immediately. Yet you know, and I know, that these ancient wrongs, these present unhappinesses, are not to be remedied in a day or with a wave of the hand. What I seem to see—with all my heart I hope that I am wrong—is a tragedy of disappointment.

The wording, one suspects, may be more that of a disillusioned Creel in 1923 than a still-hopeful Wilson in 1919—though its profound doubts were surely ones that Wilson shared. Both men were aware that public information had the power both to raise inspiring hopes and to spin entrapping expectations. Whether that power could be managed to constructive ends —and how—would soon challenge a host of propaganda analysts.

One of them, George Sylvester Viereck, observed that once the propaganda genie had escaped from the bottle during the war, there was no controlling it. For Edward Bernays, it seemed clear that the words that won the war had lost the peace. The magical new opinion-making machinery may have demonstrated its potential power, but to what eventual end?

COERCING CONSENT

Creel never really softened his candid claims to have managed American opinion. In his view, the accuracy, openness, and rationality of his wartime work were sensible means to an idealistic end. They were useful weapons in his wartime arsenal. By building credibility, they could help the public internalize what he still called "the desired compulsions."

Of course, he also realized this coercive element could—and should—be disguised. Ideally, the "compulsions" should appear to be coming from within the auditor, in the best manner of the hypnotist, the revivalist, and others who wielded the power of suggestion.

Ideally, even a manipulated public would eventually take responsibility for its conclusions, whether they were imposed or not. In this writer's experience, it was Professor Donald Fleming of Harvard University who called particular attention to the way in which such deferential techniques could disguise imperative agendas. "Suggestion by indirection," the new social psychologists had called it. Oxford philosopher T.H. Green had earlier described it as "force made to look like will."

The decision to be honest and rational did not clash in Creel's mind with the desire to dominate. For Creel, as for Ivy Lee, what was ethical and what was practical usually overlapped.

At a dinner for Creel just after the war, Secretary Baker said that "it required a stroke of genius" for Creel to trust in facts as much as he did. His trust in facts presumably implied a faith "that our democratic institutions over here would enable us to deal with information safely." What he was saying was that dealing in facts could well be *consistent* with the proper formation of public opinion, but that did not mean that the facts alone were either *necessary* or *sufficient* for achieving that goal.

Ivy Lee wanted to believe that information could be compelling because of its intrinsic accuracy. Creel, at least intuitively, seems to have known better. He would not claim that a sovereign public could carefully evaluate public information. He realized that false propaganda could find an appreciative audience among a fickle public. And the only answer in the end was Good Propaganda. The future of public opinion was moving away from the control by of the public and toward the control of the leader.

Creel's postwar reassurances were meager comfort to those who worried about the loss of public sovereignty. They reminded critics, all too clearly, that the tools he had wielded went far beyond truth, completeness, and reason. As their fears and frustrations mounted, they lashed back at those who had abused their vulnerabilities. "No effort was made to present the truth," wrote one critic. Said another, "Propaganda was a longer way to spell lie." "The word objectivity was abolished from their vocabularies," a third announced. "They All Lied," declared a headline in *The Nation*.

As was mentioned above, this reaction was reinforced by the enormous guilt trip that overtook many veterans of the publicity machinery. Heber Blankenhorn put it bluntly: "We sold Propaganda over the counter like so much meat." The noted investigative journalist George Seldes confessed, "We all more or less lied about the war. ... On Armistice Day four of us took an oath on the battlefield that we would tell the truth the rest of our lives, that we would begin telling the truth in time of preparation of war, that we would do what was humanly possible to prevent the recurrence of another such vast and useless horror."

Something had gone terribly wrong, many concluded, and even old-fashioned truth telling might not redeem the age. Creel became their symbolic target. And in response, he would start all over again with the earnest details of the Fourth of July Fake or the Three Aircraft Lies.

For a growing number, however, the real issue was not who lied to whom but rather the elusive nature of public truth itself. In a complicated world, many truths could seem two sided, full disclosure could itself be manipulative, and even objective communication could take on emotional import. One man's truth was another man's falsehood, and telling the two apart was becoming increasingly difficult. Leaders were further away in the distended society; information came increasingly from strangers, human irrationality was less easily disciplined, and whether leaders would be followed or not had less and less do with their veracity—or even their sincerity.

THE DILEMMA OF DEMOCRATIC LEADERSHIP

What the propaganda challenge clarified for many was the essential dilemma of democratic leadership. If leadership is too dominating, then public sovereignty is an illusion. If, on the other hand, a mass public is allowed to go its own way, well then, that can quickly turn into mob rule. The American Founding Fathers, wrestling seriously with this question, had pursued a rather intricate system of balanced, self-checking forces. There was no place in their new experiment for self-perpetuating monarchy, but neither should there be any indulgence of populist excesses that could so easily lead to mob rule and then right back to tyranny.

George Creel found it difficult to confront this deeper dilemma. Cleary, Madison's balanced vision had not remotely anticipated an all-powerful government information machine—forging a democratic consensus and delegitimizing criticism. What Creel simplistically fell back on was his mysterious confidence that the public shared his values. It was his way out. He was not imposing his vision since the public, at least latently, somehow already shared it.

When Creel was confronted by the House Appropriations Committee in 1918, he spent a long time recalling his work for liberal causes, going back to his support for William Jennings Bryan, his battle against child labor, and his attacks on political machines. From first to last he had been for the people, and this harmony of interests resolved for him any conflict between publicist and the public.

> I want to say that every single thing in which I have believed and every single thing for which I have fought—and this is without exception— is today law, either in federal statutes, state statutes, or in municipal charters. There is not a single advocacy of mine that has not been approved by American majorities. My crime is that I fought for these things before they became fashionable.

Here his thinking reached its logical conclusion. He would not argue as Lee did that he had set the facts before an independent public jury, awaiting their sovereign endorsement. His moral base was that he had known what was best even before the public made it fashionable. He had gotten there first.

THE ARCHANGEL WOODROW

The inherent tension between well-meaning mastery and participatory democracy also troubled the most important man in Creel's life, Woodrow Wilson. And Wilson brought to the question a wider range of intellectual and philosophical resources.

Like Creel, Wilson also assumed that a fundamental community of interest united the American public. Protecting that community required, in Wilson's view, the "purifying elements of pitiless publicity to clear away the weeds of false information." His War Message to

Congress in 1917 linked German deception to "a narrow and privileged class," one that relied on secrecy to pursue its goals. He contrasted this with the American way, "where public opinion commands and insists on full information." Later, of course, he would prescribe for international affairs the same democratic cure: "open covenants openly arrived at." "Nothing," he said, "checks all bad practices of politics like public exposure."

Of course, all of that could depend on just what was exposed and whether, in fact, the public knew enough or cared enough to think through such revelations. Did the public, at the very least, need some assistance in figuring all of these things out.? And if so, who was to provide it?

Simple exposure, Wilson realized, was only half the story. Once the garden was weeded of false information, Wilson did not trust the tender shoots of "truth" to natural processes alone. He was much too impressed—and had been all his life—by the public's inherent vulnerability, its inconstancy, its ignorance, and its fragmentation. From an early age he was preoccupied by the need for strong, positive leadership, and he prepared himself tirelessly to rally and unify opinion through the awesome power of language.

In the later words of the iconoclastic H.L. Mencken, Wilson was the "Archangel Woodrow," a Moses and a Messiah, dealing in "greasy and meaningless words" and "reducing all the difficulties of the hour to a few sonorous and unintelligible phrases." Mencken's diagnosis was extreme:

> He knew better than they did how to arrest and enchant the boobery with words that were simply words and nothing else. ... He wasted no time upon the heads of his dupes, but aimed directly at their ears, diaphragms and hearts. ... The important thing is not that a popular orator should have uttered such vaporous and preposterous phrases, but they should have been gravely received for wary years by a whole race of men, some of them intelligent.

The ultimate fault for Mencken lay more with the enabling public than with the momentary leader, an analysis that has important continuing relevance. In moments of leadership crisis, it has been said, it is not enough to replace the demagogic leader unless one can also replace or reform his "base," his trusting public.

Evidence of Wilson's preoccupation with the power of words can be found at every hand in his life and writings. At times he seemed to place more trust in words than in reality. His biographer Arthur Link describes his "early fascination" with the "manipulation of language," manifested in talks before childhood clubs, fantasy sermons emulating his preacher father, and his debate and oratory competitions at school. At Princeton he made a solemn covenant with his friend Charles Talcott "that we would drill ourselves in all the arts of persuasion, but especially in oratory ... that we might have the facility in leading others into our ways of thinking and enlisting them in our purposes." He dreamed of becoming the "American Gladstone."

A controversial study of Wilson by the diplomat William Bullitt (with what appears to have been minimal assistance from Sigmund Freud, who was credited as coauthor) adds a similar observation. "He had a passion for words, and cherished them for their own sake, for their sounds, caring more for the expression of a thought than for its substance." This reliance on words, the authors claim, was "the neurosis which controlled his life." In periods of strain, he would turn obsessively to bursts of oratory. When the war came, he gave enormous attention to finding language that would both justify and win it. His Senate adversary, Henry Cabot Lodge, tellingly complained about "the general idea that seems to run through this war that we can fight it with language."

Wilson's scholarly writings, drawing heavily on European elitists like Walter Bagehot, reflected his fear of scattered responsibility and favored a strong executive who would set out "the arguments required to determine political action with such force and effect that they really should determine it." With Edmund Burke, he asked that "what is right should not only be made known, but made prevalent." Most significantly, he agreed with Henry Maine that "the will of the people consists in their adopting the opinions of one person or a few persons."

Long before most of his contemporaries, Wilson had moved beyond nineteenth century myths about a sound and sovereign public. His critique of a perpetually ineffectual Congress, his preference for a parliamentary system, and even his 1897 attack on nominating conventions reflected a similar concern. They weakened accountability, he said, and produced "leaderless government." In 1898 he wrote that good leadership required the ability to "master multitudes" through "verbal persuasion." "Statesmanship," he said in a new 1900 introduction to his landmark book *Congressional Government*, "must replace government by mass meeting." He took some cheer from his hope that the Spanish-American War had strengthened presidential authority.

In his *Constitutional Government in the United States* of 1908, Wilson promoted the power of a president to organize "a concert of thought." The president's is "the only national voice in affairs. Let him win the admiration and confidence of the country, and no other single force can withstand him. He is irresistible." In a speech at St. Louis in 1909, he declared that the day of multiple leadership was destined to give way to the "leadership of one leading person." Eliminating direct election of a plethora of officeholders (the long ballot) became "an obsession with him," Arthur Link concluded.

As president, Wilson was quite certain that if the public disagreed with him, then the public mind must be changed. "We are not governed by public opinion in our conclusion," he said. "I want to do what is right, whether it is popular or not." He desired, he said, to lead the country "to a single way of thinking."

To that end, Wilson revived the long-lapsed tradition of delivering his Annual Message to Congress in person (something Theodore Roosevelt said he wished he had thought of doing). He claimed to know little about advertising techniques, but he clearly understood their potential. He found able technicians like Creel, Joseph Tumulty, and others to help him "fix the attention of the people on this protest of mine in a way that will give it the greatest possible emphasis." He could also be secretive, endorsing more censorship than Creel. He resented rival suitors of the public, particularly journalists, whom he criticized continually.

Even as the war ended, he expressed his desire "to keep the matter of propaganda entirely in my own hands ... I regard nothing as more delicate or more intimately associated with the policy of the administration than propaganda." He felt no embarrassment in using a word that many had already come to see as a decidedly pejorative one.

Wilson met with Creel an average of three times a month during the war, and the two exchanged almost daily correspondence. The committee in turn helped create a veritable cult of Wilson and his Fourteen Points. His Flag Day address of 1917 was reprinted almost seven million times and was carried by Boy Scouts to millions of American doorsteps, with the youngsters instructed to ask recipients to pass it on to friends. Almost half of the Four Minute Men talks, it has been estimated, revolved around Wilson or his speeches.

By temperament, training, and experience, Wilson earned his place as America's foremost self-aware propagandist, "the great generalissimo on the propaganda front," as Harold Lasswell put it in 1928. He and Lenin "were the champion revolutionists of the age. ... Such matchless skill as Wilson showed in propaganda has never been equaled in the world's history ... Wilson brewed the subtle poison which industrious men injected into the veins of a staggering people."

Wilson's efforts to square his faith in dominating leadership with the values of democracy were similar to Creel's. They centered on the claim that he spoke for public opinion even as he led it. But Wilson took a further step by distinguishing the unstable public he led from the profound public he represented. It was not that the old sovereign public had disappeared. Through a leap of faith that can only be described as religious, Wilson legitimized his leadership by identifying it with a "real" and "more solid" opinion that lay hidden and unexpressed until he articulated it.

Where might this greater opinion be found? Wilson found the answer in a nostalgic and even mystical vision: "In the small towns of the South and West, not yet touched by mob hysteria or torn by the expansive pressures of the Great Society. Not in the fevered and seething cities but in 'the quiet places' where the genius of the people resides."

"The great voice of America does not come from the seats of learning," he said in 1910. "It comes in a murmur from the hills and woods and the farms and factories and the mills, rolling on and gaining volume until it comes to us from the homes of the common men." Although the great voice of the people was less audible and less accessible in a newly confusing age, it was not dead, provided that a great leader could somehow apprehend and express its message.

MASTERY AND DEMOCRACY

For George Creel, similarly, the best way to handle his critics was "to stand on tiptoe to see over their heads the great, grim, honest unselfish nation behind them." But it was Wilson who claimed that the voice of this greater public was actually his own voice, validating his acts of leadership even as he performed them. The strong leader, he said, must act "under the impulse of a profound sympathy with those whom he leads. … Such men incarnate the consciences of the men whom they rule."

Sir Martin Conway in *The Crowd in Peace and War* had distinguished the "crowd compeller" from "the crowd exponent." Wilson was both—in practice and in theory—and he could admit to the first role because he claimed as well to play the second. The leader may employ the arts of hypnosis, but because he spoke for the crowd and not just to it, the process was really one of auto-suggestion.

What was to stop a demagogue from claiming that his work was similarly blessed? It was a question, then as now, with an unrelenting relevance. Wilson had no persuasive answer. He could only say that in calling him to leadership, God had given him a capacity to intuit the public interest and express the public will. He spoke for the people, the demagogue did not, and he could say no more, just as Billy Sunday could only assert and never prove that the Holy Spirit had inspired his own words but not those of the false prophet.

Wilson's theological references were rooted in his committed Calvinism. He elevated transcendent values above rational processes, while enlisting the power of spiritual rhetoric as an instrument of earthly leadership.

Through a mystical identification of leader and public, the coercive acts of leadership could be made consistent with democratic values. The discovery of unreason and disorganization became not only threats but levers, and the advocate who took them into account was not exploiting public weakness but compensating for it. Through the power of language, latent opinion was made manifest and broken opinion made whole. And it was the divinely inspired leader who dominated.

Wilson was not the only leader to inspire such rationalizations. Theodore Roosevelt was similarly described by the progressive philosopher John Dewey as "the phonograph in whose emphatic utterances the people recognized and greeted the collective compositions of their individual voices." But Dewey knew he was speaking metaphorically, while Wilson seemed to be speaking literally.

The New Republic aptly described the rallying cries of Wilson and Creel as "a valiant effort of the national will, forging a new relation between the expert and the people." The comment reflected the ongoing Progressive effort to reconcile the pursuit both of mastery and democracy. The US Army draft poster reflected the same dilemma when it announced, "All patriots will. All others must." Or as Wilson explained the draft, "It is in no sense a conscription of the unwilling; it is a selection from a nation which has volunteered in mass." (Creel's observation that Americans were "coerced to be free" came from a similar place, as did his famous claim that censorship could be voluntary.) And all of this rather maddening double-talk rested in the end on a divinely inspired faith that the eloquent leader necessarily reflected the public mind.

And what if the people disagreed with the leader? Why then, that was not really the people but rather the superficial, discordant voices that must in the name of democracy be converted and returned to the fold.

Wartime exigencies persuaded many Progressives to welcome this leader-centric outlook. If dominating leadership could win the war, then it might also win the peace, as well as the struggle for social justice. It could, ideally, put power into the hands of the intelligentsia, the experts, the scientific class. If, like two fine gears, the new democracy and the new mastery could be made to mesh, then perhaps one need not ask as to which was the fundamental driving force.

It did not go unnoticed, especially after the Russian Revolution, that Marxist-Leninist doctrines embraced a similar fusion of popular energies with elitist projects. Nonetheless, the possibility that the energies of rising democracy and of progressive expertise might be surging together was an exciting, tempting prospect in many eyes.

Of course, everything changed when those gears no longer meshed. Doubts grew as the Great War dragged on, as the Wilsonian postwar dream collapsed, as the Russian Revolution soured, and as new social and economic challenges intensified. As hopes for the positive potential of propaganda faded, it became even easier to blame propaganda itself for the distorted priorities and disappointed hopes.

"*Du glaubst zu schieben doch wirdst geschoben*," Goethe had written, a maxim oft-quoted in the bitter attack on propaganda in the 1920s. "You think you are pushing but in fact you are being shoved." It was a hardheaded realization, and it created a crisis of identity for Wilsonian Progressives.

Woodrow Wilson did not survive that crisis. He fought valiantly to deny its reality. He told an audience at Pueblo, Colorado, on September 25, 1919, of his continuing confidence that people "will see the truth, eye to eye and face to face" and that the people would "always rise" to the standard their leader raised "and be led by it." But that speech, halting and tearful, marked the end of his hopes; stroke and seclusion silenced the leader's voice. His tour of the nation that autumn, which ended so abruptly in one of those small western towns in which he put so much trust, represented a great, final effort of American Progressivism to prove, by sheer force of will and word, that leader and people were still one.

Looking back on it all, George Creel also wondered whether his wartime success could be repeated in a time of growing social and economic conflict. Perhaps his moment, and Wilson's, had been uniquely right for preacher propagandists, but perhaps that moment had passed.

Creel went back to journalism after the war. He was an enthusiastic supporter of Franklin D. Roosevelt, and in 1934 he ran unsuccessfully in the Democratic primary for the governorship of California. He later felt that Roosevelt compared poorly as a wartime leader to Wilson, his hero still. Creel died in 1953.

The failure of the League of Nations campaign demonstrated for many that Wilson's strength had been the strength of his own intelligence and his own voice, not the strength of a sovereign public made manifest through him. But for an important while, at least, Wilson's voice had been widely seen as the genuine voice of America. A note that the president had received on his first wartime birthday in 1917 said it all: "I find it hard to think of you as a person, for you stand for America so absolutely in my mind and heart and are so inseparably connected with the tremendous events of the time."

The letter came from George Creel.

CHAPTER 6

The Propagandist as Educator—and Vice Versa

T he identification of leader and public allowed Woodrow Wilson and George Creel to honor both the concept of popular sovereignty and a transcendent view of leadership. They shared this outlook with many leading Progressive thinkers, whose writings often expressed a revolt against structure and artifice and a respect for democratic consent. On the other hand, these same Progressives wanted to confirm their confidence in ordering intelligence and considered direction. They invariably invoked the the concept of scientific control in their discussions, and the tension between spontaniety and science, democracy and mastery became a characteristic feature of the Progressive mind.

A 1923 book called *Popular Government* by Arnold Bennett Hall spoke insightfully of "two contradictory tendencies." One was a commitment to the "science of legislation," reflected in legal drafting departments and special commissions. The other was "a growing demand for the initiative and referendum as essential remedies to protect the public against the evils of legislative abuse." Fusing the disparate tendencies became a central preoccupation for many Progressives. Their struggle was capsulized in the title of a 1958 book by an historian of technology, David Noble. It was called *The Paradox of Progressive Thought*.

The career of Senator Robert La Follette reflected the conflict at its most intense. The Wisconsin reformer was the devoted admirer of "the quiet and hush of country life, where ... there is a wiser judgment, a truer test." At the same time, he was the ardent promoter of a significant governing role for his beloved state university. La Follette's much-cited "Wisconsin Idea" called for a creative partnership between participatory democracy on the one hand and scientific mastery on the other.

CHANGING METAPHORS AND CHANGING PERSPECTIVES

Publicity, in its "pitiless" form, seemed at first to be a promising way out of the Progressive paradox. But the First World War made it clear to many that "publicity" had not only failed in that task but had helped tip the balance in the wrong direction. Some cited, as an illustration of changing attitudes, the fact that defenders of democracy had heralded Josiah Strong as a democratic hero in 1898. Why? Because he had proposed that schoolchildren, using bicycles, should distribute informative bulletins to every doorstep as a way of counteracting the sensationalist yellow press. But these same observers had a very opposite reaction when Creel similarly sent Boy Scouts nationwide from door to door with copies of Wilson's wartime speeches. What had been a tool of reform had evolved in some eyes into a tool of propaganda.

As the direct democracy movement made its way in the hopeful prewar days, twelve states adopted laws from 1907 to 1918 that required that an official "publicity pamphlet" or "voter's textbook" be delivered to every household before each election. But when the same technique was used for wartime messages, many claimed that a trusted instrument of education had been transformed into one of manipulation.

Each new popular medium that came along seemed to trigger early bursts of enthusiasm, followed by sour disillusion. The pattern would be closely repeated in subsequent decades with the popularization of radio and television, as well as new internet and social media technologies.

The imagery used to describe these developments reflected the contrasting reactions. Bright light was a particularly popular metaphor. Progressive writers would quote Emerson: "Light is the great policeman," or Lincoln: "If you turn the light into a rat hole, it will soon cease to be suitable as a rat hole." "The powers of darkness cannot avail in the full light of day," the *Electric Railway Journal* declared as it supported Wilson's plea for "open covenants, openly arrived at."

But a reversal of that same imagery was later used to express a different outlook. The *New Republic* argued in 1921 that the eyes of the world had been "blinded by too much publicity." Its future editor, Bruce Bliven, complained in 1922 that publicity was destroying "the last vestiges of privacy, solitude and contemplation." In 1927 Walter Lippmann would condemn "Blazing Publicity" for casting its powerful beam in capricious ways.

> Our publicity machine will illuminate whatever we point it at. If we point it at the "Peaches" Brown affair, it will ruthlessly and efficiently flood the consciousness of men with swinishness. Point it at Lindbergh and it will transfigure the mundane world with young beauty and unsullied faith. ... The old adage of our salad days about the curative effects of publicity under popular government seems rather naive in this age of publicity.

A second familiar metaphor, one that Ivy Lee had popularized, referred to publicity as an antiseptic that purged the germs of wickedness. Advertising was described in the *Atlantic Monthly* in 1909 as "a great germicide." For Gerald Stanley Lee, publicity was a helpful vaccine.

> Mosquitoes and reporters vie with each other in inoculating everybody with everybody else. Every man's business is every other man's business. ... The larger advertisers have already found—that the more they advertise—the more honest they have to get.

But it is striking to see similar imagery employed a few years later to make the opposite point. Frederick Lumley began his career as a prominent propaganda analyst in 1921 by comparing "slogans" to "disease germs," against which "you cannot argue." (Ten years later he observed, "Propaganda everywhere, nor any time to think.") The controlling metaphor for George Sylvester Viereck's book on propaganda in 1929 was expressed in its title, *Spreading Germs of Hate*. Governments placed "the virus of selected information into the bloodstream of the people," he wrote; the only defense was a "serum of horse sense and humor."

Carl Sandburg's *The People, Yes* expressed a similar fear.

> Always the storm of propaganda blows.
>
> Buy a paper. Read a book. Start the radio.
>
> Listen in the railroad car, in the bus,
>
> Go to a church, to a movie, to a saloon,
>
> And always the breezes of personal opinion are blowing
>
> Mixed with the doctrines of propaganda or the chatter of selling spiels. ...
>
> The storm of propaganda blows always.
>
> In every air of today the germs float and hover.

The "germs" of propaganda continued to "float and hover" in the wake of the Great War. The reporter Neil MacNeil compared propaganda to "Spanish influenza ... highly infectious." "To go into a crowd," Sir Martin Conway had written, "is like going into a cholera village." A critic named A.P. Lipsky quoted Rudyard Kipling to similar effect:

> Not only do words infect, egotize, narcotize, and paralyze, but they enter into and color the minutest cells of the brain very much as madder mixed with stag's food at the zoo colors the growth of the animal's antlers.

Other metaphors also reflected changing sentiments. A leading 1915 advertising textbook compared publicity to electricity—poorly understood but still immensely useful. But later critics would compare it to an electrocuting current sweeping through the body politic. Ivy Lee and H.G. Wells saw publicity as a clean window glass; for George Creel in 1922 it had become a "mud screen," and for Lippmann, "a painted screen where there should be a window to the world." Chemical metaphors were popular early and late; at first, one "crystallized" or "distilled" or "condensed" or "catalyzed" opinion. But a contrary view was expressed in a much-cited *New York Tribune* editorial: "The public mind to the trained propagandist is a pool into which phrases and thoughts are dropped like acids, with a foreknowledge of the reactions that will take place."

In still other usages, the democratic court of public opinion gave way to a violent battlefield; the rule of law yielded to the rule of force. "Poison gas" was a favorite comparison. Both John Dewey and Zechariah Chafee would write about what they called "the conscription of public opinion." Frank Cobb, Wilson's confidant and Lippmann's predecessor as editor of the *New York World*, argued tellingly that wartime governments had "conscripted public opinion as they conscripted men and money. They mobilized it. ... They goose-stepped it. They taught it to stand at attention and salute." Cobb's influential address was reprinted as a US Senate document, circulated widely and even memorized by contest orators throughout the 1920s. The panic was on.

A man with a fulsome title, chief of the Morale Branch for the War Plans Division of the General Staff, Colonel Edward L. Munson, gave his 1921 book a similarly elaborate title: *The Management of Men: A Handbook on the Systematic Development of Morale and the Control of Human Behavior.* Morale, he contended, is a science "whereby mental state and human behavior can be comprehensively and effectively controlled." (Such hyperbolic claims were echoed by some as late as 1961, when a Radio Free Europe spokesperson argued, "Propaganda is a weapon in many ways far more powerful than conventional or even nuclear weapons ... whereby one by one the limbs and organs of a free society are narcotized or erased.")

Earlier enthusiasm for publicity had grown in part out of the "accountability principle"; publicity would help ensure responsible behavior. After the war, what propaganda meant for many was that those who ran the world could in fact be unaccountable. Lasswell described "an overpowering sense of helplessness" in the face of organized publicity. We are "blind pawns," he said, "duped children asking to have a card trick explained."

O.W. Riegel, a scholar who would work in government information activities during the Second World War, wrote in the 1930s about "a new nervous malady, *propaganditis*, which may be diagnosed as a paranoiac hallucination of the citizen that the whole world is conspiring to put something over on him." Harvard president James Bryant Conant admitted to a similar fear; we start out "every morning," he said, "determined that today we will not be taken in by propaganda, but by evening we find that it has fooled us." For Will Irwin, new technologies had taken society back to a time "before Gutenberg," when a small closed circle "held the sole right to know what is really going on in the world."

ELUSIVE DEFINITIONS AND INSCRUTABLE REALITIES

As invariably happens when earnest academics focus their attention on an abstract phenomenon, an unending debate broke out over just exactly how the word *propaganda* should be defined. A book on the subject could not be published, it seemed, without an introductory chapter trying to elucidate that term, and that chapter would invariably begin by first clearing away the underbrush of earlier definitions.

For some, propaganda's distinguishing characteristic was its emotional appeal; for others, it was the fact that propaganda tried to hide something, its intent, its source, or its methods. For another group, propaganda was distinctive because it had a selfish rather than a public purpose. Still others felt that the size and scope of the organizing machinery determined whether information was propaganda. The unavailability of counterinformation bothered a number of people; for them, propaganda was essentially monopolistic. And then there were those for whom the word *propaganda* simply meant "lie."

Each of these definitions seemed at once too narrow and too broad, including under a pejorative banner too many things of which others approved while leaving out still other examples that many were inclined to condemn. Painstaking attempts were made to offer abstract designations (e.g., "a systematic direction of effort to gain support for an opinion, doctrine or course of action"). Often such definitions, as Harold Lasswell discerned, became virtual synonyms for the word *communication*. "When everything is propaganda, nothing is propaganda," complained sociologist Frederick Lumley, whose postwar efforts to define the term shifted more than once before he settled on a complex five-pronged answer having chiefly to do with the quality of "veiledness."

The discussion was further confused by those who insisted blithely that propaganda should not be a pejorative term at all. To prove their point, they listed socially constructive examples and argued on that basis for an almost limitless broadening of the definition. The essayist Agnes Repplier wrote in the *Independent* in 1921 that propaganda was just "a good word gone wrong," a phrase that quickly caught on, causing Lumley to remark, "I'm not so sure that it was ever going right." In the face of all this, many gave up the battle. One man's publicity is another man's propaganda, they concluded, and that was that. Yale University psychologist Leonard Doob described many analysts as moralists trying to give ethical import to an essentially neutral term. Propaganda is involved in almost all communication, he said, including the symphony orchestra and the Chartres cathedral.

What most analysts could finally agree on was that the word should be used pejoratively and that it had to do with mass communications. What they may have missed was that the word had rather suddenly come into common usage because people saw the world in a different way than they had seen it earlier. They needed a new word to reflect new issues and new insights.

Viewed historically, propaganda signified an act of public advocacy that was regarded as improper or illegitimate, and that was all it signified. The definers were all right and all wrong; all were justified in applying the word to their particular complaints; all were wrong in raising their particular interpretations to definitional status.

Earlier chapters in this book have suggested that two underlying factors brought about the "discovery" of propaganda: a new awareness of deeply ingrained human irrationality and the new challenges of a diverse and extended society. These transformations did not happen only for a reflective "thinking" class. By the 1920s the man on the street also felt that he was out of touch and losing control, living in a world, as Lumley put it, that was "unreal, strange, incalculable."

> In a very true sense, those who live under such conditions live like the primitives surrounded, as they believe they are all the time, by inexplicable spirit-agencies which arrange and rearrange affairs according to their own inscrutable desires. Living thus, one endures as if in the house of a magician who is ever working his smart tricks and mystifying everybody. It is impossible to formulate a rational plan of living in such a world because it has ceased to be predictable; managed by propagandists it becomes wholly and absurdly unaccountable.

Propaganda makes "the social order spooky," Lumley concluded, "and thus makes society a vast, many roomed, haunted house." This was a relatively new mindset a century ago. It has not disappeared.

PROPAGANDA VERSUS EDUCATION: DRAWING THE BOUNDARY

The task of distinguishing sinister propaganda from hopeful publicity was closely paralleled by an equally fervent effort to separate propaganda from another social process that it often seemed to resemble. That process was education.

A prodigious literature reflects the effort to define the boundary between education and propaganda. It could be the line that separates children and adults, schools and the outer world, the true and the false, reason and emotion, the general and the special, the open and the ulterior, the spontaneous and the deliberate, facts and doctrines, values and techniques, or what is traditional and what is changing. The almost desperate concern to save education from the tainted connotations of propaganda was part of the reason, in fact, for the sudden popularity of the new Latin word. By collecting what one did not like under a pejorative label, one could more easily discuss and defend that which bore more respectable names.

Advancing the agenda of education was an important cause for American Progressives. Like publicity, it was a mediator between consent and control, between personal expression and social discipline. The dawning perception that publicity could turn from a tool of mediation to an instrument for control was paralleled in the literature of Progressive education.

Good education, it was argued from an early date, would avoid both anarchy on the one hand and indoctrination on the other. James Mark Baldwin, who helped found Princeton's Psychology Department, wrote in 1897 about the important "dialectic of personal and social growth," while a leading American educator, George Vincent, insisted that the individual and the social mind must grow together. Edward Ross and Graham Wallas also wrote about education as reconciling individuals with their culture, and soon the word *education* came to imply a fusion of liberty and direction.

The individual and society are two aspects of the same thing, Charles H. Cooley wrote in 1902. We must keep "always trying to see the whole in the part, the part in the whole and human nature in both," he added in 1909. To that end, he urged the construction of "local culture centers" to provide a "democratic discipline" amid the disorganizing impulses of the Great Society. His friend Charles Ellwood argued passionately at one moment for a more "natural spontaneous social order" and at the next moment for "masterful leadership."

JOHN DEWEY AND THE RECONCILING ROLE OF SCIENCE

The high priest of Progressive reciprocity, particularly in education, was John Dewey. His philosophy, strongly rooted in Hegelian dialectic, was distinguished by an enormous capacity for seeing potential cooperation where others saw combat, for insisting that what some called contradiction could become a creative synthesis. Dewey was confident that students and teachers, the public and leaders, and laymen and experts could achieve creative partnerships.

In *Democracy and Education* in 1916, Dewey spoke of the ideal educational environment as one in which the natural life of the student is expressed and shared. At the same time, however, it is a place where "the older bring the young into like-mindedness with themselves." The leader enlists "the person's own participating disposition," but "the control is inescapable." In 1918 he sounded more than a little Wilsonian as he described how democratic education, unlike the Prussian variety, produced social direction out of "heightened emotional appreciation of common interests."

Dewey's Hegelian roots served him well in maintaining this balance. Loyalty to one pole of his dialectic implied loyalty to the other; they were completely interdependent. However, it was not always easy to maintain the equilibrium, and Dewey's own rhetoric would inevitably slip a bit more to one side and then to the other.

Some of his statements seemed very permissive; leadership must never overstep its proper bounds. There must be no conscription of thought. The leader must be subservient to some larger intelligence, and policy should be tested by its capacity to "endure publicity" in the marketplace of ideas. Especially in his early writings, Dewey's emphasis was on breaking away from outmoded structures and liberating the child.

Deferring to nature, however, could only go so far. Democratic discussion must be protected against hazardous stampedes and "sheer mob hypnotism." Particularly in the period between 1910 and 1930, it became easier to discern the regulative element in Dewey's writings. The people must not be allowed to wallow in "Bryanism," he would urge. Those of higher intelligence must replace superficial "revivalists" with inspiring leadership. Yes, they must even work to "control opinion" and thus produce "intellectual and emotional unity."

In three definitive *New Republic* articles in the fall of 1922, Dewey even made a case for "Education as Religion," "Education as Engineering," and "Education as Politics," describing his viewpoint as "nothing less than a belief in the possibility of deliberate direction of the formation of human disposition and intelligence." By 1931 he was describing every teacher as "a social servant set apart for the maintenance of proper social order and the securing of right social growth." The erratic voice of popular majorities, on the other hand, was not a dependable counselor.

Dewey genuinely yearned at one and the same time both for more accommodation and for more direction in public affairs. And he finally settled on a way to handle the dilemma. To do so required an enduring and reliable guardian of the public's interests, a new source of legitimacy and discipline. That reliable underpinning would be the scientific method.

A commitment to science could provide a standard by which all public questions could be resolved and proper leadership certified. Its blessing did not derive *a priori* from the inspiration of particular leaders, as with Wilson. Nor was it legitimized by a leader's support of particular policies, as with Creel. The values it elevated were procedural ones; its ethic resided not in ends but in methods.

The much-sought-after universal truth, Dewey wrote, is a "process." It was something "relational," reflecting new structuralist understandings of language itself. The absolute was a matter of "pursuit." Truth was not a thing; truth was "adverbial." Society was never planned but always in the process of planning.

Optimally, the people would be taken in as partners with the scientific leader in a reciprocal process of investigation and discussion; both could be seen as experimenters in the laboratory of public policy. Neither the voice of the expert nor the voice of the people was "the voice of God," Dewey wrote in 1928; the two parties were partners in a noble pilgrimage.

In practice, of course, the public could be an unpredictable partner, passive at some moments and confused at others. To be sure, it could provide interesting testimony, raw material for scientific processing, but sorting out the findings would happen at a higher level. The first loyalty of leaders was not to their constituency but to science. In its name leaders could just as properly dismiss public inclinations as obey them.

Leaders who followed the scientific method were by definition operating in the public interest, whether some temporary majority endorsed them or not. By legitimizing certain kinds of authority, the scientific method resolved for Dewey the Progressive paradox.

A leader who operated without the blessing of science was what Dewey meant by a propagandist. For such leaders, it was not the fact of control that made their communications suspect but their failure to play by scientific rules. Dewey liked to describe propaganda as "unnatural," "incomplete" or "discontinuous" communication. As Charles Ellwood would put it, "intelligence is evil only when it is partial."

No leader could be perfectly scientific, of course, and Dewey's distinction between propaganda and education could often seem a bit blurred. If one had an overriding scientific purpose, for example, that in itself might turn what might seem like an act of propaganda into an act of education. In newly revolutionary Russia, he initially observed, propaganda was ostensibly aimed at "the universal good of a universal humanity." In such a case, he hopefully speculated, propaganda and education "are more than confounded, they are identified."

Dewey was also ready to acknowledge, in cases where the goals were endorsed by science, the legitimacy of irrational appeals, endorsing the use of art and poetry to kindle emotion and of selection and emphasis to gain attention. These persuasive devices, he felt, were essential to proper education, whether of a child or a public.

DOUBLE-TALK AND DISCUSSION

Those who still elevated individual spontaneity and public sovereignty, however, were much more inclined than Dewey to distrust top-down influencers. Dewey's concept of education, like the work of the Committee on Public Information, seemed doubly dangerous to them because it so often disguised its impositional agenda.

Dewey, of course, denied that scientific control might often blur into coercion. Rigorous scientific discipline would always reconcile the interests of the leader and the led. To some ears, it could sound like double-talk. For example, he would say that democracy "will have its consummation when free social inquiry is indissolubly wedded to the art of full and moving communication." Other Progressive educators, however, were less nimble in holding on to both poles of Dewey's dialectic.

In this regard, Christopher Lasch's later, influential appraisal is well worth considering. While Dewey repeatedly complained that his ideas were being distorted, Lasch said:

> The evident ease with which they were distorted did not cause him to reexamine the ideas themselves. He might at least have reflected on the possibility that they contained ambiguities which made them peculiarly susceptible to misinterpretation, if misinterpretation was in fact what was taking place.

Interpretations of Dewey's work did, in fact, vary widely. On one side, some used his appreciation for childhood spontaneity to justify the most permissive of educational experiments. Others went the other way. A notable example was the reconstructionist educator George Counts, in his 1932 call upon the nation's schools to help build a new social order. American education must "become less frightened than it is today at the bogies of imposition and indoctrination ... [it must] deliberately reach for power and then make the most of [its] conquest."

Many followed Dewey in embracing the potential of group discussion to produce scientific decisions while welcoming diverse inputs. An influential movement with roots in the 1920's gave the very word "discussion" an almost sacred status. The movement also drew heavily on the work of Cooley, Ross, and Wallas, as well as on models of community discussion like the Des Moines forum and the Danish folk high schools. Political theorists like Mary Follett and Seba Eldridge also captured the ardor of the movement, and so did newly emerging speech and communication departments at many colleges and universities.

The discussion movement aimed to democratize cooperative decision-making, but the iron hand of discipline could often be discerned within that velvet glove. A Wellesley College professor of rhetoric, A.D. Sheffield, wrote a book in 1922 called *Joining in Public Discussion*, part of organized labor's Workers Bookshelf series. The effective discussion leader, he asserted,

> must begin mastering the technique of discussion by which the whole group is maneuvered into cooperative thinking and speaking. The real technicians of modern democracy are those who win insight into the forces of thought and feeling that can be touched into activity when people sit down together. The student of discussion, therefore, should picture a deliberative meeting as a sort of field of magnetic forces wherein his mind can conspire with other minds to organize socially advantageous currents.

His use of words like *maneuvered* and *conspire* did not give comfort to those who believed in democratic consensus.

Also revealing was a 1928 manual circulated far and wide by the YMCA. It was called *The Process of Group Thinking*, written by Harrison Sacket Elliott. Discussion, he said, was the best possible weapon against the propaganda menace, so exhilarating, said Elliott, that "it is hard to believe that this is not some new and subtle propaganda." Many thought it was.

MARIA MONTESSORI AND SCIENTIFIC EDUCATION

Perhaps the most influential of the new educational theorists of that era (and ours) was an Italian, Maria Montessori. Her landmark 1909 book centered on *Pedagogia Scientifica*; the first of many influential English editions appeared in 1912. For Montessori, the scientist must be "the worshipper of nature," and the educator must likewise worship the spontaneous child. The teacher's obligation is "to guard that spiritual fire within man, to keep his real nature unspoiled and to set it free from the oppressive and degrading yoke of society." A good teacher virtually disappears from the child's consciousness, working always to release the person who lies dormant in the child's soul.

> In such a delicate task, a great art must suggest the moment, and limit the intervention, in order that we shall arouse no perturbation, cause no deviation, but rather that we shall help the soul which is coming into the fullness of life, and which shall live from its own forces.

So far, so good. But then, in the very next paragraph, the goal of all this accommodation is (rather astonishingly) revealed.

> When the teacher shall have touched, in this way, soul for soul, each one of her pupils, awakening and inspiring the life within them as if she were an invisible spirit, she will then possess each soul, and a sign, a single word from her shall suffice; for each one will feel her in a living and vital way, will recognize her, and will listen to her.

Through "indirect control" the teacher would make "an interior conquest."

> "Now listen," we say. "A soft voice is going to call your name." Then going to a room behind the children and standing within the open door, I call in a low voice, lingering over the syllables as if I were calling from across the mountains. This voice, almost occult, seems to reach the heart and to call to the soul of the child. Each one as he is called, lifts his head, opens his eyes as if altogether happy, then rises, silently seeking not to move the chair, and walks on the tips of his toes, so quietly that he is scarcely heard.

It is difficult to avoid the impression that this could be Svengali all over again—a Svengali who applied the lesson of the scientist—that one adapts to that which one seeks to control—as well as the lesson of the propagandist—that one has one's strongest influence over a subject who believes he is free. Montessori called this "indirect" or "spontaneous discipline," even as Charles Cooley had written about "a free discipline" or "a democratic discipline." And of course, it was George Creel who would insist that the American people in wartime were being "coerced to be free."

For some critics, in the words of *Trilby*'s Laird, its potential was "just too terrible to think of."

* * *

Montessori had a large American following. By 1913 more than 100 Montessori schools had already been opened in the United States. Alexander Graham Bell and his wife launched a Montessori school at their Canadian home. S.S. McClure published Montessori's articles in *McClure's Magazine*.

One of her most enthusiastic disciples was the man who headed New York's Montessori-based House of Childhood, Carl Byoir. It was Byoir who described the Montessori method to the National Education Association in 1912 as a heightened respect for individuality. He was also remarkably confident that out of the apparent chaos "there arises an almost perfect discipline."

In 1917 this same Byoir became George Creel's right-hand man at the Committee on Public Information, the "multiple director" who had "grown up" with the committee, according to Creel: "I used his organizing ability in division after division, moving him from one to the other, and, whether the activity was domestic or foreign, he showed equal skill in giving it efficiency, force, and direction."

After the war, Byoir achieved immense success as one of the "big three" pioneers of professional public relations. Byoir was responsible not only for a parade of business publicity successes but also for not-for-profit projects such as Franklin D. Roosevelt's famous "birthday parties" to promote the anti-polio campaigns of the March of Dimes.

In time, however, Byoir became a polarizing figure, accused of deceiving American opinion on behalf of the notorious Machado regime in Cuba. He was also the man who, with Ivy Lee, brought the public relations field its own worst publicity when his counseling relationship with the Hitler government was revealed in 1934—a relationship that made Lee's flirtation look mild by comparison.

The big three figures in the public relations world also included Ivy Lee, of course. And then there was a third figure, a trenchant thinker and writer who would work hard to take the field in a rather different direction. His name was Edward L. Bernays, and we turn next to his long and remarkable story.

CHAPTER 7

Edward Bernays and the Engineering of Consent

"Find New Profession in Caruso Suit Trial," a *New York World* headline announced in 1920. Profits from the Italian singer's American tour were in dispute, and Caruso's press agent had been summoned to testify. When asked for his name and occupation, the twenty-eight-year-old witness had replied, "Edward L. Bernays, counsel on public relations." The headline writer had alertly found that response more interesting than the trial itself, and as the counselor himself would later observe, "Subsequent events have proven him right." The episode foreshadowed a career that would bring as much attention to Bernays as it did to his clients. It epitomized his ability to dramatize both the originality and the respectability of his work.

For neither the analogy to legal "counsel" nor the term *public relations* could Bernays claim authorship. Ivy Lee, after all, had suggested, under the title "Modern Lawyer" in 1904, that "this age has created new professions." The term *public relations* had been used in the late nineteenth century and was frequently invoked before 1910. However, the combined phrase "public relations counsel" was Bernays's invention, and he built around it both a philosophy and a calling.

In this instance, as in many others, what was implicit in the thought and practice of Ivy Lee became explicit with Bernays. Lee's half-formulated suggestions became Bernays's philosophical expositions. If Lee's role was to sell public relations to the business establishment, Bernays wanted to sell public relations to the public.

"He thinks he is a pioneer because he is so self-conscious," Leonard Doob wrote somewhat skeptically of Bernays in his text on propaganda in 1935. But in a field that understood itself poorly, Bernays's self-awareness was itself an accomplishment.

He was self-conscious about the resulting recognition as well, valuing testimonial letters that his publishers solicited. "You burst your way into virtual terra incognita—the forming of human opinion—and plotted maps which will guide men for a long time to come," wrote Erwin Canham, editor of the *Christian Science Monitor*. Harvard psychologist Gordon Allport told him, "Important principles of public opinion, persuasion, and communication were first enunciated by you." Professor Max Lerner referred to Bernays's "seminal mind," and eminent news commentator H.V. Kaltenborn testified, "He has done more than any other man to teach the world how to analyze and evaluate public opinion."

Bernays fittingly called himself a "propagandist for propaganda." When *Editor & Publisher* and *Printers' Ink* stepped up their campaign against press agents in the 1920s, he appointed himself as publicity defender at large and took out newspaper advertisements to educate the country. By the 1930s *Time* magazine would refer to him as "U.S. Publicist Number One." In 1935 a publication called *Advertising and Selling* said he was "widely regarded as the greatest press agent alive." "Bernays had more to do with developing acceptance for public relations than any other half dozen persons," said public relations executive William H. Baldwin in 1948.

"To men of my generation," wrote Professor Thomas Cochran in 1966, "you were the symbol of post–World War I public relations." Bernays's cousin, Martin Freud, recalled how American visitors in Europe would tell him (as well as his father, Sigmund) that these European relatives had "no idea" how great Bernays's influence was in the United States and that he might even become president someday.

FROM THE "HIGHER HOKUM" TO THE "SCIENCE OF HUMANICS"

Edward L. Bernays was born in Vienna of Jewish parents on November 22, 1891, and brought to New York a year later. He attended private schools and was sent by his father—a grain exporter who valued rural life—to Cornell Agricultural College, where he graduated in 1912. He became involved in 1913 in the torrid debate over *Damaged Goods*, a French play dealing with venereal disease, raising money to help produce the play in New York.

From medical play promotion to the promotion of plays in general and then of musicians—so ran his early career. He worked for Diaghileff's Ballet Russe and Nijinsky and helped artists like Caruso acquire what Bernays called "gilt by association." He went to work for the Committee on Public Information in 1917; he accompanied Wilson and Creel to Versailles in 1919 and returned disappointed that their "great experiment" had not prevailed.

His wartime experiences forced him to think of publicity in new ways, he later recalled. To be sure, he had once pictured himself (poetically) as an ordinary space grabber, "thinking … thoughts of plastering the city in half an hour, With twenty-four sheets and large heralds, And a page or two in all the dailies." But that image quickly lost its appeal.

Journalist Bruce Bliven testified later to Bernays's success:

> When I became old enough to know what was going on in the world
> … a press agent ranked about with a tramp printer—a rootless qua-
> si-vagrant and, all too often, an alcoholic incompetent. You have
> done more than any other single person to banish this figure from the

American scene and to replace him by the expert in public relations, a solid citizen, respected because he is respectable and earning so much that the whole Senior class of every School of Journalism seems to want to move en masse into that occupation.

While Lee's preferred role model was the prominent business lawyer, Bernays's ideal was the academic intellectual. His parents had come from distinguished European families; the obligations of their traditions were impressed on young Edward. His most prominent relative, of course, was his uncle Sigmund Freud (actually his uncle twice-over, since Edward's mother was Freud's sister, and his father's sister was married to Freud).

Freud's influence on Bernays did not stem from an intimate personal tie. Rather, his uncle's celebrity became important to the nephew for its own sake; it gave him both a personal model and a public talking point. Public relations skills, he wrote in 1944, are like "bedside techniques, as delicate and complex as those utilized by the psychiatrist." He called his work "the new science of humanics."

Bernays's writings are replete with what Irwin Ross would call his "wistful yearnings for scholarly distinction." (The journalist also commented on how Bernays's language could resemble "clods of jargon dropping like huge pillows which cushion the mind against anxiety.") Bernays pursued respectability for his profession by tracing its origins to the priests and scribes of ancient Egypt and Sumeria. Even as his first book was being readied for publication in 1923, "I decided one way to give the term professional status was by lecturing on the principles, practices and ethics of the new profession of public relations at a university." He gave a short course at New York University that spring and promoted the extension of such courses to other schools. He later claimed that twenty-one institutions of higher learning offered public relations courses in 1945, a number that had doubled by 1948 and doubled again ten years later.

At times, of course, Bernays himself, perhaps for shock value, would talk about "the science of ballyhoo." But it remained for him a science, nonetheless. In order to promote the sale of paper cups in the 1930s, for example, he organized a distinguished Committee for the Study and Promotion of the Sanitary Dispensing of Food and Drinks. The committee even published a scholarly bibliography, the purpose of which, he said, was "to establish authenticity for our effort."

He maintained a close rapport with many academicians. One was Harwood Childs, a Princeton professor who in 1934 produced of one of the first bibliographies devoted to public opinion and who was editor for many years of the *Public Opinion Quarterly*. Childs acknowledged Bernays as one "who is among those whose genius enables them to bridge the chasms between the laboratories of academic endeavor and the world of practice."

His eager intellectual yearnings were mocked by many. P.T. Barnum might be regarded with a certain amusement, but Bernays's academic pretensions seemed too intense to be smiled away. Critics—nervous about the power of propaganda to begin with and doubly frightened by the specter of Freudian magic added to the brew—assumed the worst. An early reaction came from Dean Eric Allen of the University of Oregon's new School of Journalism:

> The despised "press agent" of an earlier day has developed first into the "publicity man" and then into the "promotion" expert. ... He is a real problem; scolding will not eliminate him. He is respectable. After a course in sophistry, necessitated by his self-esteem, he comes to regard himself as ethical, and his own careful statement of his functions exhibits him as a useful member of society. He worked for the government and helped win the War.

With his "pinch of poison," said Allen, he represented "the beau ideal of gutter journalism." When Bernays's own *Crystallizing Public Opinion* appeared in 1923, the response was often cynical. "The public relations counsel, of course, is merely our old friend the press agent, more or less ill at ease in his strange habiliments of psychology and the minor sciences," said the *New York Times*. In *The Nation*, Ernest Gruening (a future Alaska senator) wrote a widely noticed review under the title "The Higher Hokum." The public relations counsel, he said, is "the shabby underpaid fellow who sought to worm a little free space out of the newspapers by devious ways, to the nth power. Today, equipped with his title and other accoutrements of respectability, he steps forth as a superdiagnostician of the public mind."

Beneath the headline "Ex-Farmer Fertilizes America's Mass Mind," the *New York World-Telegram* portrayed Bernays a decade later as the "Montaigne of Mammon," the "Baron of Ballyhoo," "a prophet to the people for the profit of his clients." *Fortune* concluded in 1939 that the title "public relations counselor" seemed to be "the most preposterous pretension of them all."

The New York *Evening Telegram and Mail* called Bernays's new profession "a lineal descendant of the circus publicity man." An advertising man, E.E. Calkins, termed the public relations counsel "the old press agent with a high hat." The much-heralded city editor of the *New York Herald Tribune*, Stanley Walker, described the new profession as "the refuge of the incompetent." Walker offered a fascinating list of additional euphemisms:

> public relations counsel, publicity advisers, advocates at the court of public opinion, good-will ambassadors, mass mind molders, fronts, mouthpieces, chiselers, moochers, and special assistants to the president.

The contemporary term *spin doctor* might be a useful addition to the list.

Reactions to Bernays's memoirs in 1965 revived the skeptical assault. Marvin Barrett offered this vivid appraisal in the *Reporter* magazine. "Public relations for the most part still remains a trick rather than an art, a figment rather than an idea. [It is] a ferry shuttling eternally between the shores of profit and social usefulness, with the cargo always loaded in favor of the return trip."

What explains this never-ending parade of exercised denunciations? Surely, one reason was a genuine fear of the power that a sophisticated publicist might wield. And some criticisms seemed those of writers who were frustrated press agents themselves (judging from the overripe style of their writing). Bernays himself blamed the hostility on "a cultural time lag," confident that he would be vindicated eventually. "Quite a change from 'The Higher Hokum,'" he smiled as he paged with this writer through two impressive volumes of warm, testimonial letters presented to him on his seventieth and senty-fifth birthdays in 1961 and 1966. (He would live to be 103 years old.)

More than most of his fellow practitioners, Bernays took on clients from all across the commercial, political, and cultural spectra. While he worked for Dodge Brothers, General Electric, United Fruit, Westinghouse, and the Bank of America, he often recalled with more relish his clever campaigns for less prominent clients. On behalf of the luggage industry and the millinery trades, he battled the trend to skimpier and simpler flapper fashions. When sales of Venida hairnets dropped during the bobbed-hair fad inspired by the celebrity actress Irene Castle, he helped restore them to favor by stressing their hygienic function for cooks and waitresses. In similar ways he promoted greeting cards, velvet, jewelry, and artificial flowers.

Communications and publishing ventures were also among his favorite clients, including Hearst's *Cosmopolitan* and *Good Housekeeping*, the *Ladies' Home Journal*, the new publishing house of Boni and Liveright, and even William Paley of CBS and Henry Luce of Time Inc. during their early, experimental years. In the 1940s he aided *McCall's* and helped Henry Wallace revitalize the *New Republic*.

He was also called in by governments and governors, by candidates and commissions. He never tired of recalling his advice in 1914 that Tomas Masaryk should declare Czechoslova-kian independence on a Sunday in order to receive greater play in the world's newspapers. "But that would be making history for the cables," Masaryk is supposed to have objected, causing Bernays famously to respond, "But it is the cables which make history."

In the early 1920s the enterprising young publicist set up a "show business breakfast" for Calvin Coolidge to counter the "weaned on a pickle" image that plagued the president. He lectured at the Industrial College of the Armed Forces during the Second World War and advised the governments of India, Vienna, and East Orange, New Jersey. He was briefly retained by Prime Minister Ngo Dinh Diem of South Vietnam, but the relationship ended when his advice was ignored. He established a foundation to promote Anglo-American relationships and was continually selling pet ideas such as a cabinet secretary for public relations or "a Joint Canadian–United States Board for Mutual Understanding."

With his wife and partner, Doris Fleischman, he decided in 1946 to divide his time equally between paying and public service clients. As early as 1920, the couple had helped publicize the Atlanta convention of the National Association for the Advancement of Colored People, the first ever held in the South. They were longtime advisors to Roger Baldwin and his

American Civil Liberties Union. In 1931 they plotted strategy for the Committee on the Cost of Medical Care in its confrontation with the American Medical Association.

Bernays told members of the American Nurses Association to call themselves "registered nurses" because, when prostitutes were arrested, they frequently identified themselves as "nurses." He challenged the American Association of Museums to help mobilize the nation's "psychological front" in wartime. He campaigned for feminism and eugenics, for freer trade and for Sigmund Freud, and for the Social Science Research Council. In later years, his causes included the political campaigns of Adlai Stevenson and the campaign to help Caryl Chessman avoid capital punishment.

He also made a significant splash with a project to save the sycamore trees along the Charles River in Cambridge, Massachusetts. In an earlier, similar effort to save a stand of sycamore trees on East 63rd Street in New York City, he teamed up with a neighbor, the exotic dancer Gypsy Rose Lee, which led to a considerable bit of happy punning on the words "strip tease" and "strip trees."

Bernays consistently urged his wealthy business clients to share their wealth and not just their words, to become *pro bono publicos*. Even his frequent critic George Seldes conceded that, while Bernays was the "plutogogue of plutogogues" (the word was a cross, one assumes, between *plutocrat* and *demagogue*), he "usually hires himself out for the better causes."

CRYSTALLIZING PUBLIC OPINION

Bernays made the quest for social progress a major theme of his first book, *Crystallizing Public Opinion*, in 1923. Later, when the book was republished to honor Bernays's seventieth birthday, exuberant well-wishers attributed to it an historical significance that even its author may not have perceived. Harold Lasswell, for example, reported that *Crystallizing* had been a volume of "unusual importance," one he had assigned to his students for many years. "In this rapidly changing world not many men have published a book dated in 1923 that can be read without wincing to this day," he wrote. The historian Daniel Boorstin called it "one of the most important books in the social history of our age." Another celebrated academic, Peter Odegard, ranked Bernays's book with Walter Lippmann's *Public Opinion* and John Dewey's *The Public and Its Problems* as one of the three "great pioneering works in a field that still defies those who want simple answers to complex problems."

Bernays designed *Crystallizing* as a sequel to Lippmann's study, a book, he said, that had "made a great dent in my life." He followed Lippmann in describing "the art of creating consent among the governed" as the most significant development of modern times. He wrote not only about "creating consent" but also of "molding" and "converting" the public conscience; he borrowed from Le Bon, Trotter, and Martin in praising the power of symbols to move the crowd mind.

As he referenced these concepts, he began to scrape against the familiar problem of top-down direction versus bottom-up consent. His early choice was to scurry back to the safe ground of saying that genuine consent must be willed by the public, whenever he found himself looking into an autocratic abyss.

To that end, he cast the new publicist less as a leader than as a broker, a sort of traffic cop, standing at the center of the communications web and keeping information flowing smoothly in all directions. If poor information created what he would call a "Tower of Babel," then better communication could foster consensus. "What they [the people] want and what they get are fused by some mysterious alchemy," he wrote. "The press, the lecturer, the screen and the public lead and are led by each other." To the familiar riddle, Does public opinion obey the press or does the press reflect public opinion?, he gave this answer: "The two interact upon each other, so that it is sometimes difficult to tell which is one and which is the other." A free marketplace of competing propagandas, he concluded, would somehow protect everyone from anyone's arbitrary influence.

All of this could sound a bit like the old-fashioned arguments of Ivy Lee, falling back on a comforting faith in public dependability. When asked much later to compare himself to Lee, he said that his message went beyond "pitiless publicity." It was no longer enough merely to clarify a client's image in the public's mind. "The client must also learn to perceive the public more accurately." Public relations was a two-way street, a matter of "interpreting the client to the public and the public to the client." The view was not all that different from John Dewey's Hegelian sense of interacting dualities.

What Bernays sensed—to a degree matched by few of his contemporaries—was the demanding nature of this second task, perceiving and interpreting the public. He feared the growing reality of social disorganization. But he also felt that, properly understood, abnormal social fragmentation could be transformed into reliable social cohesion. Consensus and harmony were natural social conditions; the public relations operative did not create harmony so much as discover it.

Even in his extremely candid discussion of opinion control in his next book, proudly entitled *Propaganda*, in 1928, he emphasized the need to find a "common denominator" between the seller's idea and the consumer's interest. "You must find a link between your desire to be a leader and their desire to welcome you," he told a business group in 1936. In his later years he would proclaim his personal unwillingness to accept any project unless he could first locate the place where his client's interest overlapped with that of the public. What was less clear was whether other talented publicists could be counted on to exercise the same self-restraint.

At New York's Cooper Union in 1938, Bernays delivered a substantial address on "Private Interest and Public Responsibility," again arguing the need for interest groups to "conform," "adjust," "integrate," and "bow" to the public will. He would argue the same point in his book *Public Relations* in 1952:

If our competitive society had developed at an even rate, if everything had meshed itself in a pattern of perfection, we might not need
public relations, because our interrelationships would be perfect. But
in the flux of a democratic society, there are maladjustments between
individuals and groups, on the one hand, and society as a whole or
sections of it on the other. In this society, public relations has emerged
as a form of social statesmanship.

Open competition in the marketplace of ideas would evoke this underlying harmony, he
theorized. To this end, he popularized the aphorism that "the only cure for propaganda is
more propaganda." He even identified "freedom of propaganda" as a critical civil liberty in
his appearance on *America's Town Meeting of the Air*. Just as Ivy Lee argued that whatever the
public could be led to believe must be rational, so Bernays hoped at times that whatever the
masses could be brought to accept would be to their benefit.

By no means did this mean for Bernays—as it sometimes did for Lee—that the publicity
man was a mere curtain puller or window pane. From the start he recognized that the public
relations profession must work hard to discover that magic place where public and private
interests coincide.

Crystallizing Public Opinion included, therefore, a perceptive presentation of what Bernays called the techniques of "salesmanship," including the mechanics of distributing
information, the principles of mass psychology, and his "Segmental" and "Indirect" strategies for achieving social goals. In such passages he slipped more easily into talking about the
vast "power" of public relations and about public "dependence" on special pleaders.

Bernays was reluctant, however, to join Lee in applying the court of law analogy to the
practice of public relations. He had been tempted by the analogy early on. "What the lawyer
does for his client in the court of law, we do for our clients in the court of public opinion,"
he intoned in 1920. But he later concluded that the legal analogy underplayed the need
for talented publicity specialists. As he explained in 1923, "In law, the judge and jury hold
the deciding balance of power. In public opinion, the public relations counsel is judge and
jury because through his pleading of a case the public is likely to accede to his opinion and
his judgment."

HAVING IT BOTH WAYS

Bernays, like so many others, wanted to have it both ways. The title of first book, *Crystallizing Public Opinion*, reflected that desire. In a single word, *crystallizing*, he was able
to express both his impulse to shape opinion and his respect for public integrity.

To "crystallize" something, the dictionary tells us, is to cause it to take on a definite
and concrete form, but one that is "characteristic," that is, established by nature. This

crystallization, however, can be facilitated by an outside agent. The metaphor captured beautifully a delicate intellectual balance.

A careful Charles H. Cooley had used the word in 1909 (when he defined public opinion as a "crystallization of diverse but related ideas"). The word had appealed to Walter Lippmann. Randolph Bourne had worried that war fever would prematurely "crystallize" dangerous public sentiments. The same convenient term had been used by many other writers.

Bernays and his publishers arrived at that word, however, only after lengthy discussion. The book was originally known and even advertised as *In the Court of Public Opinion*, but the author decided this was "not dynamic enough." The same deficiency also disqualified its suggested replacement, *Informing Public Opinion*. In that case, as someone then said, "why not simply try *Forming Public Opinion*?" But that possibility was "too cynical" for the author's taste.

The middle road led to the word *crystallizing*, and like Goldilocks in the story of the Three Bears, Bernays found this alternative "just right." It recognized that "there are certain *a prioris* in the public mind to begin with" and, more than that, "it had no negative connotations."

A history of American attitudes toward public opinion could be built around the words people have used through the years to paper over the tension between leadership and consent. On one side are those who have spoken about "informing" opinion, or "understanding" and "heeding" it, perhaps of "expressing" or "encouraging" or even of "gathering" and "discovering" it. On the other side one hears about "creating" public opinion or "manufacturing" or "directing" or manipulating" or even "welding" it. In between came words with the potential to blur the issue, to imply that public opinion has its own configuration and at the same time to show that it is malleable, that it can be "influenced" or "steered" or cultivated" or "shaped." Among Bernays's favorites were the ideas of "molding" and "mobilizing" opinion or perhaps the idea of "accelerating" and "directing" it. Later ("when we became a little more courageous," as he would candidly recall to this writer) he would settle on the phrase "the engineering of consent." He found that phrase to be "more dynamic, more meaningful, more definitive, more truthful" than even "crystallizing." However, in 1923 the word was *crystallizing*.

Nature will have its way, but man can assist nature. Or, as the economist Simon Patten said, in a mystifying phrase that Bernays understandably found helpful: "Nature will care for progress if men will care for reform."

One admiring correspondent (by the name of Joost A.M. Meerloo) shared his personal appreciation for what Bernays had done in finding such a careful and "difficult" word as *crystallizing* to describe his role. (But when Meerloo, a Dutch psychologist and later a professor at Columbia University, authored his own study of totalitarian "brainwashing" in 1956, he carefully chose a very different title, calling the book *The Rape of the Mind*.)

PROPAGANDA: TELLING IT THE WAY IT IS

Sigmund Freud acknowledged receipt of his copy of his nephew's *Crystallizing Public Opinion* coolly and aptly: "As a truly American production it interested me greatly." He was more enthusiastic, however, about Bernays's bolder second book, published in 1928 and defiantly entitled *Propaganda*. "I picked up your new book not without misgivings that it might prove too American for my taste," Freud wrote to his nephew. "However, I found it so clear, clever and comprehensible that I can read it with pleasure."

Bernays was tired of hedging and balancing. Public opinion in the 1920s had proved to be neither intelligent nor independent. With an evident sense of release, Bernays decided to tell it the way it is—and this time he pulled no punches.

> The conscious and intelligent manipulation of the organized habits and opinions of the masses is an important element in democratic society. Those who manipulate this unseen mechanism of society constitute an invisible government which is the true ruling power of our country. ... We are governed, our minds are molded, our tastes formed, our ideas suggested, largely by men we have never heard of ... a trifling fraction ... who pull the wires which control the public mind, who harness old social forces and contrive new ways to bind and guide the world.

Universal literacy had once been seen as an answer to this danger:

> But instead of a mind, universal literacy has given us "rubber stamps," rubber stamps inked with advertising slogans, with editorials, with published scientific data, with the trivialities of the tabloids and the platitudes of history, but quite innocent of original thought. ... Propaganda is the executive arm of the invisible government. ... The important thing is that it is universal and continuous; and in its sum total it is regimenting the public mind every bit as much as an army regiments the bodies of its soldiers.

And all of this in just the first twenty-five pages.

Of course, Bernays's answer for all of this propaganda was more and better propaganda.

This fear of invisible masters to which he appealed was amplified markedly in 1928 by the highly visible investigation of public utilities conducted by the Federal Trade Commission (FTC). The hearings began by exposing the utilities' vast, unsuspected networks for "publicity" and "education." *New York Times* reporter John Carter described these networks as a vast "system of deceit," so insidious, he wrote, that "they might swing an election." The *Times* article, entitled "Unseen Empire," was one of a series of worried exposés of invisible conspiracies working to undermine US democracy.

One part of the machinery was a private publicity bureau called E. Hofer and Sons. Founded in 1912 in Salem, Oregon, the firm had reportedly been distributing strongly conservative articles and editorials to 14,000 of the nation's 20,000 newspapers, and many editors had been running them as if they were their own copy. Hofer argued that because "the advocates of socialism never sleep," businesspeople, including utilities executives, must help "stabilize the mass consciousness and crystallize it against the adoption of radical or unsound propositions." Not unfamiliar words at the time, nor today.

A rash of books had focused on the utilities' "propaganda mill," and so did the congressional investigation. One former publicity man, J.B. Sheridan of Missouri, contributed an anguished confession. He had personally "just about changed the entire trend of economic and political thought in the United States. That's all!" How? "Give us the child at seven years old, and we care not who educates him; thereafter, he will be ours." But the thrill wore off. He finally came to see his employers as "cheap, lying politicians." He now was burdened with guilt. He wrote to a friend in 1927: "Damn it all, John, they never can make hypocrites and cowards of all the people. T' -ell mit 'em." Less than three years later, Sheridan committed suicide.

One of the consequences of the FTC investigations was a move by the American Association of University Professors to set in order the academic house, which had been implicated in propaganda efforts. E.R.A. Seligman headed a prestigious committee that reflected the fear of "hiddenness" in its report in 1930: "The fundamental principle, therefore, in any question of propaganda, is that of full, complete, entire, and honest publicity—publicity as to the source, publicity as to the motives, publicity as to the methods, publicity as to the objective." Again, the answer to bad publicity was a lot more publicity.

Harvard political scientist William Bennett Munro published a bitter, well-argued attack in 1928 on the same target, calling his book *The Invisible Government*. He spoke for many as he described the arena of public discussion as "a great stock exchange," where ideas are bought and sold by amoral propagandists. "If I thought the voice of the people was the voice of God," he announced, "I should be sorely tempted to become an atheist." This seemingly antidemocratic assertion came from the immediate past president of the American Political Science Association.

Munro traced the phrase "invisible government" to a speech by the Republican statesman Elihu Root in 1914; it had grown in popularity in the 1920s. Bernays used it frequently in *Propaganda*, and one reviewer accurately described the Munro and Bernays books as mirror images, both describing the same phenomenon but one (Munro) despairing and the other (Bernays) rejoicing.

Arguing that the voice of the people is the voice of God leads to "political sterility," Bernays concluded. Yes, public and private interests should eventually coincide, but this might happen only within the consciences of "the intelligent minority." "Ours must be a leadership democracy administered by the intelligent minority who know how to regiment and guide the masses," he said. "Small groups of persons can and do make the rest of us think what they please about a given subject." To Benjamin Disraeli's comment, "I must follow the people. Am I not their leader?," Bernays responded, "I must lead the people. Am I not their servant?"

The word *leader* was being pressed into service more and more, a useful way to spare democratic sensibilities while still affirming the propagandist.

The *Bookman* published an even livelier Bernays volley in 1937 under the provocative title "The Minority Rules." It opens by recalling Jefferson's faith that the country was made for the common man. But the common man, it continues,

> shows no sign of giving three whoops in East New York whether it was made for him or not. Caesar leads him along by the nose. ... If this means anything at all, it means that anyone with enough money, or enough influence, can lead the public where he will, [can] stain the public mind to a desired tint. ... The common man is content to let his affairs be run for him; let the intelligent see to it that they do the running.

He gave the same elitist advice to the academic community in the *American Journal of Sociology*: the title was "Manipulating Public Opinion: The Why and the How." One reason "why," he allowed, was that manipulation "safeguards the public from its own aggressiveness."

Later Bernays would regret what he called his "naiveté" and recant at least a part of this outburst. "Only the brashness of youth could explain the optimistic use of so baleful a word as 'manipulating,'" he would write in his memoirs. However, "despite the title or maybe because of it, public relations became a subject of interest in social-science circles."

That interest was not confined to social science circles, however. For 1929 was also the year of Bernays's most famous publicity campaign—the one, he said, which "kicked me upstairs." The campaign was designed to mark the Golden Jubilee of electric light. The celebration climaxed at a meeting in Dearborn, Michigan, bringing together President Herbert Hoover, Henry Ford, and Thomas Alva Edison, now eighty-two years old. The result for Bernays was a tidal wave of publicity. Some was favorable. Much was not.

Bernays became a national symbol of the propaganda menace. His *Crystallizing* book had earlier been compared to Machiavelli's *The Prince*, and that same comparison was often used to describe his new *Propaganda* book. Historian Henry Pringle described him in *American Mercury* in 1930 as "a stern realist who operates upon the demonstrable theory that men in a democracy are sheep waiting to be led to the slaughter." An *Atlantic Monthly* profile attributed to him the notion that the consumer is "utterly disorganized and helpless." Leonard Doob's seminal book in 1935 saw him "exploiting" the public and "making himself and his whole profession the arbiters of social change." Said Everett Dean Martin, "When Bernays and his kind have finished their work, an American Tacitus will be able to write, *Republica Americana delenda est.*"

Bernays would later describe his comments "about mass mind control and invisible government" as his own mistake. But at the time he could not restrain his enthusiasm for the arts of publicity. They operate, he said in 1935, in "every phase of our activity." "Average men throughout the ages learned that they do better in following their leaders than by following their own lead," he told a Depression-era audience.

He proposed to the American Political Science Association in 1935 the establishment of a cabinet secretary of public relations. "Bizarre" was the appraisal of this idea in the newly popular *Time* magazine, citing the proposal's potential for untoward censorship.

Consistent with Bernays's confidence in wise elites were his worries about the growing popularity of market research and public opinion polls. While he used such surveys in his own work, he did so more to shape tactics than to set goals. "We are no longer led by men. We are led around by polls," he complained at one point. In response he called, most presciently, for the licensing of pollsters and for training the public to view polls skeptically.

The Second World War did not dilute the elitist element in Bernays's rhetoric. Far from it. In fact, it encouraged a flurry of military metaphors. His article in the *Saturday Review* in 1942, for example, suggested that "the use of ideas as weapons must go hand in hand with our military planning and economic strategy." He advised the Industrial College of the Armed Forces of the need for "psychological ramparts ... as strong as our physical ramparts" and for "a psychological general staff" with an authoritative role similar to other military commanders. The goal was to "stockpile public opinion."

His speech at Western Reserve University in 1943 made the same point regarding "psychological warfare ... we always get back to the leaders no matter where we start." In 1946 his concern about public vulnerability led him to argue for limited suppressions of freedom of speech.

One trigger for Bernays's midcentury concern about public gullibility was the appearance of an unabashed racist, Senator Theodore Bilbo, on television's *Meet the Press*. Such incendiary voices might light a prairie fire, he warned. The public could not protect its own self-interest, he insisted in an interview with this writer in 1968. Most people cannot identify their congressional representative, he pointed out. The idea of reliable public consent was an unrealistic invention of Enlightenment French philosophers. Modern psychology and sociology have taught us that most public sentiments are imposed by others.

Such views led him to the phrase "the engineering of consent." From the 1940s onward, he would use those words as the title for speeches, articles, and even for a book that he edited in 1955. The term established for him, on the control versus accommodation spectrum, a position toward which he had long been aspiring.

When he later said to this writer that he regretted the use of the term *propaganda*, it was mainly because of its public relations costs; it scared too many people. The word *engineering* was more acceptable. The engineer, after all, must work with the forces and materials he is given. He was fond of a line from George Bernard Shaw that made that point: "The function of the statesman is to express the will of the people in the way of a scientist."

The engineering concept had appealed to a surprisingly long list of earlier writers. A *Bookman* article in 1906 had complained of the "secret engineering of sentiment by means of news made for the purpose." Edwin L. Earp, from the Drew Theological Seminary, praised a similar process in a 1911 publication called *The Social Engineer*. The influential philosopher about crowds, Georges Sorel, had been trained as an engineer, and his classic *Reflections on Violence* in 1910 discussed the engineering of dissension. Gerald Stanley Lee, whose folksy poems and essays appealed to Bernays, described advertisers as "attention engineers" in 1916, cabinet officers as potential "news engineers" in 1919, and in 1920, the president as "an engineer in folks ... an engineer of the will of the people" with a "huge national derrick up on the White House."

Dewey wrote of education as engineering in 1922; Frederick Pierce saw auto-suggestion in the same terms. A book called *Manhood of Humanity, The Science and Art of Human Engineering* appeared in 1921. In 1917, Ivy Lee referred to the "publicity engineer" and so, even earlier, did a small 1911 volume called *Ads and Sales* by Herbert Newton Casson.

> The man who directs the publicity work of a great corporation, if he does his work well, has just as much right to the title of "engineer" as the man who plans a subway or a bridge. He, too, has to deal with opposing forces. He has to measure and calculate and construct, and he is none the less a builder because the structure he creates is made of Public Opinion, rather than wood and steel.

FOUR METHODOLOGIES FOR THE SOCIAL ENGINEER

Bernays wrote proudly about his practical engineering techniques. He organized his comments under four headings: the mechanics of information distribution, a concern for applied psychology, understanding the larger cultural matrix, and the use of indirection and circumstance.

Simply getting the word out was the first step. As he had told Masaryk, "It is the cables that make history." He said in his first book that three men warned that "the British were coming," but we remember only one. "Did Revere make history," he asked, "or did Longfellow?" It grieved him that foundations would spend a million dollars on a research project and have no resources left to save the product from an obscure burial on dusty library shelves. You could build a better mousetrap, he said in 1952, "but the world will not beat a path to one door unless that door has high visibility."

The second of Bernays's tool sets was applied psychology, manipulating the levers of human personality. He rejected what he called "reaction psychology," alluded to the work of the crowd psychologists, dropped in references to Sigmund Freud, and embraced Lippmann's concept of stereotypes.

What levers might be used to awaken "underlying emotions"? In 1927 he identified simply "sex, gregariousness, the desire to lead, the maternal and paternal instincts." One of his most noted publicity campaigns grew out of such psychological insights. His charge was to promote Lucky Strike cigarettes among women in 1929, and in preparation he consulted A.A. Brill, the famous Freudian psychologist. Brill told him that smoking is both a sublimation of oral eroticism and a symbol of freedom. Accordingly, Bernays staged a feminist-style march along New York's Fifth Avenue on Easter Sunday, billing it as a protest against yet another sex taboo. Ten debutantes carried aloft their "torches of freedom," and the spectacle produced controversy—and publicity—across the land.

He followed up with a whirlwind campaign to make green the fashionable color of the day so that women would favor the green "Luckies" package. He set up a Green Ball, a Green Luncheon, and even a Green exhibition of paintings at New York's Reinhardt Galleries. He pressured designers, buyers, and fashion editors to follow the trend, and he largely achieved his goal, he said, in just six months.

In the 1930s Bernays returned to Brill for more advice concerning cigarette advertising. This time he learned that cigarettes are a phallic symbol, and that "every normal man or woman can identify with an ad in which a man offers a cigarette to a woman."

After the Golden Jubilee of Light, he theorized that Thomas Edison's heroic stature resulted from the public's need for a father substitute. Yet such talk of phallic symbols and father substitutes was relatively rare, especially for the nephew of Sigmund Freud. He spoke about hidden motivations but rarely discussed them in psychoanalytic depth.

A third area of tactical concern was what Bernays called "the cultural matrix." He enjoyed sociological analyses, including those of W. Lloyd Warner and Helen and Robert Lynd. "Democratic society is made up of almost an infinite number of interest groups," he wrote in 1948. "Men turn for guidance to the leader of groups of which they are members." It was to this multitude of opinion leaders, therefore, that publicity counselors should address their appeals. He contended in 1943 that there were exactly 788,257 such interest group leaders in the United States. The key to unlocking the intricate machinery of "interlocking" and "interlacing" interests, he said, was effective interest group leadership. Most advertising was "overly homogenized," he said. One pursued social order by adapting to the disorder.

Opinion leadership would become the dominating theme in a famous 1955 study of *Personal Influence* by Elihu Katz and Paul Lazarsfeld. Opinion leaders could provide a cushion—perhaps even a filter—that would save the public from dangerous, distant manipulations. Such analyses supported the feeling—in academic and popular circles alike—that the vogue of mass propaganda in the interwar years had been overblown.

For Bernays, opinion leaders were the very means through which a good propagandist should work. He was somewhat put out, in fact, when Katz and Lazarsfeld's important book did not cite him as a source in that he felt he had discussed the idea with Lazarsfeld in earlier conversations. Lazarsfeld's response was to contrast what he saw as Bernays's intuitive theories with his own empirical demonstrations of how opinion leaders played their inter-mediating role.

The fourth and perhaps most important methodological category for Bernays was what he called the strategy of "indirection." The "think green" campaign was a classic example, as were devices such as the hygienic promotion on behalf of hairnets, the encouragement of a diversified wardrobe in order to sell more luggage, a health campaign designed to replace the metal drinking cup with cups made out of paper, and the propaganda for more public highways that he waged for Mack Trucks. Another example was his successful soap sculp-turing contest, set up in schools on behalf of Ivory soap.

In each instance, the commercial payoff was significant for the client, but the commercial purpose was relatively obscure. The public could elect to wear green clothes or carve up soap or vote for a new highway without reflecting on what this might mean for American Tobacco or Procter & Gamble or Mack Trucks. Such appeals—like appeals to the subcon-scious—allowed the publicist to bypass the public reasoning process. The strategy was ideal for a time when people were increasingly skeptical, and even cynical, about overt public advocacy and tired of "organized nagging," in the words of journalist Elmer Davis (who also served as director of the Office of War Information during the Second World War). In such a climate, "the most indirect kind of indirection" (the phrase is Bernays's) could be a useful tool.

The editor of the *Atlantic*, Ellery Sedgwick, told Bernays, "My picture is this: you see life like a billiard table. Direct shots are barred, and your nimble ball caroms continually off the cushion of circumstances, affecting the situation not at first but at second hand."

Bernays described his indirection strategies simply as "the creation of circumstances" that would have a favorable impact. Words could be fickle, but "actions cannot lie." He embraced what his friend Harry Blackstone, the great magician of the interwar years, called "the science of misdirection." "If the leaders of the world would turn their talents to a little more magic," Blackstone had said, "there wouldn't be so much hurt and misery. Politicians are nothing but magicians anyway." A prominent scholar of propaganda, William W. Biddle, saw it the same way: "Propaganda must focus the mind so that the thought of rejection does not occur," he said. Suggestion accomplished this end by internalizing the imperative. Indi-rection did so by misdirecting the audience—or even by distracting it. An indirect strategy did not require that the evident interests of client and public should overlap. The common link that brought two parties together could be a marginal concern for each of them.

One need not tell the public any more of the story than is necessary to engage some corner of its interest. One need not worry too much about "the whole truth," since "there is no whole truth, only selective truths." (One might wonder whether "selective truths" are similar to "alternative facts.") If the publicist could achieve a coincidence of interests between client and public on a marginal matter, then he might use that as a pivot point for turning the public onto a more significant, albeit unanticipated path.

"A HOBBESIAN WAR OF SMILES"

Indirection had one potential in common with the other techniques we have examined: what seems to be adjustment can turn out to be manipulation. Whatever the technique involved, Bernays's central advice was to "bow to the inevitable." And the reason one bowed was to reach for the lever of influence.

It was no longer enough merely to tinker with natural processes or to give nature a slight push toward its own predetermined ends. Social engineers should advance their goals boldly through the exploitation of natural processes. If Cornelius Vanderbilt had said that the public should be damned, and Lee had urged that the public should be informed, Bernays would always say that the public should be understood. But he said this as a social scientist who knew understanding can be a road to control.

His most manipulative moods could produce his most cooperationist language. His book *Propaganda* emphasizes phrases such as "friendly agreement" and "give and take"—and he meant them. He recognized the growing mistrust that greeted distant communicators in an increasingly estranged society, and his response, like that of some colleagues, was to elevate the role of selflessness and sincerity in the arsenal of public persuasion.

"Public relations," Robert Heilbroner wrote in 1967, "is Dale Carnegie writ large." In his runaway best seller, *How to Win Friends and Influence People* (1936), Carnegie, a former food salesperson, outlined a technique of self-advancement built on smiles and sincerity. Bernays himself would later write a Carnegie-like article under the title "Do People Like You?" Yet another voice was quoted to the same effect, suggesting that friendship is "a drop of honey which catches the heart, which, say what you will, is the high road to his reason." In this case the quotation was credited to Abraham Lincoln, cited in a 1920 book called *The Buying Impulse and How to Lead It*.

In *The Social Engineer* in 1911, Edwin L. Earp described his ideal leader as "a minister of personality." "The social engineer," he said, "must master the art of making friends." Another exuberant writer and cleric, Gerald Stanley Lee, melded the language of coercion and cooperation in 1919: we must always be "big brothers of the people," he wrote, "battering the enemy with cooperation, being impregnably, obstinately his brother, by piling up huge, happy citadels of good-will." Jesus Christ was again the model, for he taught an "unconquerable and bewildering way of fighting ... turning the other cheek is a kind of moral jiu-jitsu." If the propagandist was in truth a mesmerizing Svengali, he was quickly finding new disguises.

In 1921 a public utility spokesperson defined the art of publicity as one of "aggressive courtesy" and "cumulative cooperation." He advised his associates to "join the thank you club." Public relations, said another practitioner, was "merely human decency which flows from a good heart." "Try to be a nice guy," advised the irrepressible Dexter Fellows, publicity director for the Ringling Bros. Circus, who was known as "the master of ballyhoo." All the world, he said, loves "a gentle liar."

As this essay is written, the longest-running musical play on Broadway is *Chicago*, ostensibly set in the 1920s and reflecting its Jazz Age aura. Its definitive moment focuses on a super-slick lawyer who tells his vulnerable (but guilty) client not to worry about the murder charges against her: it's all about entertainment, he says. He then begins to sing "Give 'em the ol' Razzle Dazzle." The lyrics end with the words: "And they'll never get wise." The continuing resonance of the lyrics may help explain the musical's enduring popularity.

The historian David Potter would link the rise of self-interested cooperation to the disappearance of the open American frontier.

> Where wealth is gained more readily by organizing and manipulating other men than by further raids upon nature, the traits of personality, persuasiveness, attractiveness—personality! it is called—have become essential competitive equipment, and the "other directed" man has forged to the front.

As personal contact with an intimate community declined, surface impressions—words and gestures, symbols and myths, smiles and shoeshines—would fill the stage. An historian of popular religious sentiment, Donald Meyer, has described the process as a "Hobbesian war of smiles." In Meyer's view, winning friends in order to influence people could often mean replacing reality with harmonic fantasies. Purpose was lost in personality. The message was lost in the medium.

The quality of being well liked would be the badge of effectiveness for Arthur Miller's quintessential salesman Willy Loman, who told his sons in *Death of a Salesman*, "It's not what you say, it's how you say it. ... Be liked and you will never want." Miller summed it up in the final scene of his 1949 stage play: "Willy was a salesman ... a man way out there in the blue, riding on a smile and shoeshine. And when they start not smiling back—that's an earthquake."

Strong as the *Salesman* dynamic became, however, Bernays resisted its excesses. He never became an exuberant Carnegie, much less a woeful Loman. Yes, he was fascinated by questions of technique, but his overriding concern was the practical end result. He bitterly rejected what he saw as Herbert Hoover's mind-cure approach to the Great Depression; "self-delusion," he called it, a substitution of communication for content.

Similarly, the international Kellogg-Briand Peace Pact of 1928 was often described as a meaningless, linguistic gesture. John Dewey related the pact's reliance on affirmative language to the new, positivist appeals of Christian Science. On the other hand, Bruce Barton predictably liked the pact—and suggested that the missing ingredient was an advertising campaign to support it.

Bernays rarely mistook style for substance. He developed the trappings and tokens of the other-directed man, but—to use the jargon of a later day—he was other-directed for inner-directed reasons. He may have helped produce the great "American Salesman," but he remained the great "American Engineer."

THE QUEST FOR PROFESSIONAL SELF-DISCIPLINE

Bernays's great goal in his later years was to underscore the gravity and integrity of the public relations profession, especially as thoughtful Americans worried increasingly about totalitarian propaganda.

In 1935 Sinclair Lewis published *It Can't Happen Here*, a novel describing a fascist takeover in America. A leader of the fictional coup was the chief demagogue's press agent, Lee Sarason, who later would grab the dictatorship himself before being assassinated in the White House "in his violet silk pajamas." Lewis designed Sarason as a composite of well-known "PR" men, explicitly comparing Sarason's skill in "the greatest of all native American arts, the art of publicity" with that of Bernays. "New York" and "Jewish" were listed among Sarason's possible origins (so, to be sure, was Georgia). Like Bernays, the fictional Sarason had wandered Europe in his youth. He had "lost his trust (if any) in the masses during the hoggish nationalism after the war: and he believed now only in resolute control by a small oligarchy. In this he was a Hitler, a Mussolini."

Lewis's wife at the time, the noted journalist Dorothy Thompson, had compared the techniques of Hitler and Bernays as early as 1932. (She had once tangled with Bernays over an article she had written about his uncle.)

In 1933 Bernays was informed, to his embarrassment, that Joseph Goebbels was using his book, *Crystallizing Public Opinion*, as "a basis" for propaganda campaigns in Germany. The subsequent revelations about the Lee and Byoir connections with the Nazis further increased his vulnerability, though he had turned down an invitation to work for Germany's Dresden fair. He was targeted by an old critic, Ferdinand Lundberg, for having himself "decked out in the regalia of democracy like a bawd in the garb of virtuous woman." Most propaganda, Lundberg continued, "is nothing more than an unpalatable dish served with appetizing sauces. If people could taste the dish without the sauce, they would, nine times out of ten, simply vomit." Bernays critics were lashing out ever more recklessly now, and Bernays adjusted his rhetoric.

Initially, he stopped using the word *propagandist*, while admitting that he had once used it rather "proudly." Almost astonishingly, but astutely, he said that he "would never have put out a book with the title *Propaganda* if I had known what the word would come to mean in the next several years."

By the late 1930s a phrase he preferred was "Public Education for Democracy." When asked much later if he had changed his mind about anything over the course of his career, he would speak of the notions of mind control and invisible power, which had become so "frightening." "Boy, I dropped all that!" he would tell this writer.

Others would not drop the matter—then or later. The major Bernays biography, published in 1998 by *Boston Globe* journalist Larry Tye, was entitled *The Father of Spin*, approaching Bernays from an appreciative but skeptical perspective. In 2005, ten years after his death, Bernays's decidedly aggressive book *Propaganda* was republished, reinforcing an image he had tried to minimize. It was positioned as a book of historical importance, a "manual" on propaganda, or, as New York University professor Mark Crispin Miller put it in his reproachful introduction to this new edition, "propaganda for propaganda."

Although Bernays adjusted his vocabulary, he stood by the values of strong leadership, working even harder to legitimize its exercise. Both the New Deal and the Second World War helped confirm his faith in human engineering. But he found it increasingly difficult "to find ideas that still stand for leadership and that are not utterly valueless."

Among other things, he turned up the volume on the notion that publicity techniques could further the cause of democracy in an increasingly autocratic world. "Public relations counter-acts the tyranny of every sort." He made the point in a 1940 manual called *Speak Up for Democracy: What You Can Do* and even in his role as publicity director for the New York World's Fair in 1939. "The world is in a chaotic state. It needs leadership."

"Any one of us can change the political and social actions of his fellow Americans," Bernays announced in a book with the apt title *Take Your Place at the Peace Table* in 1945. Elites still largely controlled masses in Bernays's model, but he stressed now that anyone could be a leader. Elitism itself might be democratized.

The will to control was of primary importance, but what Bernays now was furthering were democratic objectives. As George Creel had put it in defending wartime propaganda, if he was coercing people at all, he was coercing them to be free.

To his credit, Bernays no longer fell back on the enigmatic and paradoxical phrases that he had sometimes used to "muzz over" the leadership/consent dilemma. Earlier escape phrases had included his 1927 claims that people might be "unified, propagandized, and standardized into independence." Or equally implausibly: the engineering of consent must come "from all" (1941). Or: an opinion engineer works by "outmaneuvering his opponent in the public interest" (1947). "He acts as a channel for the will of the group, draws it out, encourages it, gives it direction and force to make if effective."

Bernays thought too clearly, however, to be long content with such convenient reconciliations. He would finally come to a realistic position that relied, straightforwardly, on the righteousness of the leader himself. The social engineer must discipline his own behavior. In the final analysis, it was the decent motives and good sense of the self-policing opinion molder that would anchor Bernays's philosophy of responsible publicity. His answer would focus on the moral capacity of individual human leaders.

His most important legacy, he felt, would be his impassioned campaign for the professionalization of public relations. In its pursuit he promoted legislation in the New York State Assembly for the licensing of practitioners. (It foundered on fears of government "meddling.") He worked to create an ethics-oriented professional association, even while he later eschewed such efforts if they seemed to be born out of a "promotion psychology." He never joined the Public Relations Society of America because, he felt, "its standards are not sufficiently professional." Others agreed with him. Irwin Ross's overview of the industry, *The Image Merchants*, tells of protracted industry conferences during the 1950s that came up with bad or weak codes with no means of enforcement. Ross's diagnosis was that most practitioners would regard as "suicidal" any attempts to enforce ethical canons.

Nonetheless, Bernays continued to advocate for the right kind of professionalization, pushing for rigorous programs of training and state licensing. He worked to develop a professional literature, a heightened awareness of the industry's collective history and mission. He was prepared to be patient. It had taken centuries for law and medicine to attain their current professional status and structure, he observed, and he was confident that his profession would also overcome the "cultural time-lag."

In his own ruminations he would wrestle with questions similar to those of legal ethicists. For example, should a counselor try to reform or reject a client of whom he does not approve? He regretted the work he had done for tobacco companies before he knew about the health hazards of smoking, and he was consulted on later efforts to discourage the habit. (Typically, he proposed the removal of ashtrays from public gathering places.) Would he approve of another counselor taking on a client he had rejected? Yes, he decided; he would not himself work for Barry Goldwater or Ronald Reagan, but he would approve of someone else doing so.

But his interest in such questions was not contagious. The right kind of industry-wide professionalism remained for him an unrealized dream. He might have been tempted now and then to agree with an old *New Yorker* comment that public relations often served as a road of social mobility for "third-rate" people. Or as Neil MacNeil put it, the greatest danger for Bernays may be that he "tempted inferior men to follow him."

The impulse to professionalization may have fed in part on Bernays's quest for personal distinction and academic credibility. But, as was the case for Ivy Lee, it also had a larger function. For Lee, the analogy to the legal profession helped him sell public relations to the business world. As Bernays saw it, the analogy to academics, medicine, and law could help make public relations safe for democracy.

PRIVATE RESPECTS AND THE PUBLIC GOOD

More than most commercial propagandists, Edward Bernays acknowledged the undemocratic potentials of modern information management. His writings can be viewed as a constant struggle to "find the due place in the modern democratic scheme for this new propaganda." But the struggle was always difficult. He was able to speak now and then in the language of Jefferson and Locke, but his heart was Hamiltonian. He was dedicated in the end to progressive mastery and constructive consolidation, to finding a new sense of order in a time of "chaos."

Bernays introduced his autobiography in 1965 with this quotation from John Milton:

> That grounded maxim
>
> So rife and celebrated in the mouths

Of wisest men; that to the public good

Private respects must yield.

Social harmony must be forged by skillful leaders, or as Croly had put it, "by heroes and saints." Bernays was skeptical about "direct democracy" reforms such as open primary elections or the popular referendum, but he nonetheless valued the dream of democratic community and hoped that disciplined leadership could restore it.

He occasionally speculated about a general will or group mind that might be subjected to Freudian introspection. But even so, it was the expert analyst who made self-analysis work. Bernays believed that the ideal analyst was the enlightened publicist.

The "grounded maxim" of Milton's that Bernays set out at the beginning of his memoirs announced it was "the public good" that the wisest men, the expert analysts, should advance, not "private respects." But the sad reality, then and now, was such maxims themselves could be misleading.

The passage in *Samson Agonistes* from which Bernays—with the help of the *Oxford Book of Quotations*—secured this idealistic quotation had, in fact, been Milton's way of warning against those who audaciously talked about "the public good" as a way to disguise their private ambitions.

The words are Delilah's. As the Bible story recounts, she has just betrayed her husband, Samson. As he slept, she had shorn him of his hair—the source and symbol of his power. As a result, he had been taken captive by his Philistine enemies and finally blinded. Now she comes to Samson in his anguish to confess her "rash but more unfortunate misdeed." And she blames it on her scheming tempters: magistrates and priests "ever at my ear," who were rationalizing her betrayal of Samson by claiming "that to the public good/private respects must yield." It was in fact the "bad guys" whom Delilah, Milton—and Bernays—were quoting.

Samson can only reply: "These false pretexts and varnish'd colours failing, / Bare in thy guilt how foul must thou appear."

More than most of his contemporaries, Edward L. Bernays understood the dynamics of a new age of public unreason and distension and the potentials in such a time for organized publicity. All his life he had tried to envisage those publicity potentials as "yielding" to the public good, but hard reality kept bursting through his visions.

Even as he completed his autobiography in his seventy-fourth year, the poetic words he chose to epitomize the respectability of his creed and his craft served also to demonstrate their inescapable dangers.

CHAPTER 8

Walter Lippmann's Unblinking Realism

One of Edward Bernays's favorite writers was a man who shared his realistic outlook. Yes, the two writers both argued, the people should be respected by understanding leaders, but the responsibility for human progress finally rested upon responsible elites.

The writer whose work so impressed Bernays was also a New York City native. The two men were born ten years apart, both of German Jewish parents. They grew up in highly cultured, upper-middle-class families on Manhattan's Upper East Side. Both attended Dr. Julius Sachs's School for Boys; both entered journalism after graduating from Ivy League colleges. Both worked for the government as propagandists during the Great War, and both reacted to that experience by writing widely influential books that appeared within a few months of each other in 1922 and 1923. Bernays was Sigmund Freud's nephew and his representative in North America. His counterpart was among the first Americans to use Freudian psychology in writing about public affairs.

Both men commented frequently on how the nature of human experience had been transformed in a newly distended and highly impersonal society. Perhaps one reflection of this very fact was that, despite so many overlapping experiences, places, associates, and interests over so many years, Edward Bernays never met his counterpart, Walter Lippmann.

***

Lippmann was born in New York City in 1889, the precocious only son of a prosperous, widely traveled German Jewish family. He went through Harvard University in three intense years, deeply influenced there by the thinking of William James, George Santayana, and most particularly, Graham Wallas. His studies focused on art history; he was president of the Socialist Club. He spent a fourth Harvard year as an assistant to Santayana, wrote briefly for the liberal *Boston Common*, and then joined Lincoln Steffens at the muckraking magazine *Everybody's*. In 1912 he became secretary to the Socialist mayor of Schenectady, New York, but quickly grew disillusioned with the inability of socialism to educate a recalcitrant public. He returned to addressing a more elite audience, publishing two attention-getting books, *A Preface to Politics* in 1913 and *Drift and Mastery* in 1914, while also becoming a founding editor of the *New Republic*.

In wartime, he helped shape President Wilson's Fourteen Points proposals and then joined the Committee on Public Information, focusing on psychological warfare against Germany. He briefly assisted at the Paris Peace Conference but felt himself useless and returned disconsolately to America. He quickly published two more books, *Liberty and the News* in 1920 and the landmark book *Public Opinion* in 1922, and he became editorial page editor and then editor of the *New York World*. He then settled into a long career as a leading political columnist. He died in 1974.

As his eminent biographer, Ronald Steel, would write in 1998, "He was not only America's most distinguished journalist but a confidant of statesmen, an author of learned books, and a guru on nearly every public issue. ... He had the mind of a scholar and the pen of a reporter."

Lippmann's childhood and college friend, Carl Binger, recalled how he loved to read aloud in his room at Harvard's Weld Hall from Swinburne: "From too much love of living, From hope and fear set free, We thank with brief thanksgiving, Whatever gods may be." The lines represent Lippmann's attitudes throughout his career, his determination to give no hostages to illusions, to derive meaning not from the wanderings of the imagination but from a stern appreciation of fact. If some currents were irreversible, if some obstacles unavoidable, he would accept reality and make what he could of it.

This outlook was evident in his first book in 1913.

> Our primary care must be to keep the habits of the mind flexible and adapted to the movement of real life. The only way to control our destiny is to work with it. In politics, at least, we stoop to conquer. There is no use, no heroism, in butting against the inevitable. There is always some choice, some opportunity for human direction.

One inevitable reality was human irrationality. He cited Milwaukee's Socialist mayor, Emil Seidel, who argued that smart social planners must "go into competition with the devil," harnessing basic human drives for good purposes. He was already impressed by Freud. "Instead of tabooing our impulses we must redirect them. Instead of trying to crush badness we must run the power behind it to good account," he wrote. In his second book, *Drift and Mastery*, he continued in a similar vein: "What civilized men aim at is neither whim nor taboo, but a frank recognition of desire, disciplined by a knowledge of what is possible."

In introducing a popular later edition of *Drift and Mastery*, historian William Leuchtenburg stressed the contrasts between these first two Lippmann books, the first submitting to the reality of unreason, and the second seeking to master that reality through scientific insight. Another scholar, Charles Forcey, similarly reported that sometime between the two early books, "Lippmann abandoned the anti-scientific Bergsonian world of drift and fantasy for the more prosaic scientific experimentalism of John Dewey."

Such commentary has contributed to an exaggerated impression that Lippmann had been "converted" to science by influencers such as Graham Wallas. But in fact, whatever changes there were in emphasis, both of these early volumes worked hard to interrelate adaptation and control. *A Preface to Politics* tells its readers that they must be creators, conquerors, and inventors, "aggressively active towards the world," going beyond the routinized supervision of a President Taft in favor of the "new guidance" of men like Roosevelt. They must be ready to move mountains "as engineers do, when mountains stand in their way." By the same token, *Drift and Mastery* devotes its final chapter to reminding new scientists that they must also "serve" the spiritual and the aesthetic dimensions of life. Dreams and emotions, imagination and desire, can be raw materials for scientific practitioners.

> Before the scientific spirit can reach its full bloom, it will have to acquire an honest sense of the role that fantasy plays in all its work. ... Mastery, whether we like it or not, is an immense collaboration in which all the promises of today will have their vote.

This dual vision, including the prospect of "an immense collaboration," was shared, as we have seen, by many intellectuals of the Progressive period, including advocates for the discussion movement and for progressive education. The key, as Lippmann put it, was to be both "masterful" and "humble." He praised the example of Montessori; like Plato and Machiavelli, he said, she began her work by dealing with humanity as it really is. An ideal politics, Lippmann wrote, "would be like education—an effort to develop, train, and nurture men's impulses." The scientific spirit should be one with "the spirit of education; not to produce a row of respectable automata, but to draw out of each child the promise that is in it," much as the artist releases an imprisoned image from a block of marble. Just as Dewey's ideal teacher honored both childhood impulse and social imperatives, so Lippmann's statesman helped his society look "inward at desire and outward at fact."

What did shift some from Lippmann's first book to his second was the precise set of realities that had to be accommodated. New Freudian insights about human irrationality were a major focus of the first book; Wallas's description of newly complex social structures dominated the second.

The old "Nation of Villagers" had lost its way amid new social complexities, Lippmann emphasized. Like Don Quixote, the public often moves "in a world that has ceased to exist." Uprooted man, wrote this child of Manhattan, lives now at second hand, hungering for the genuine country life where "words still taste of actual things, where contact with sun and rain and earth and harvest turns the simple prose of the day's work into poetry for the starved imaginations of city-bred people."

> We live in great cities without knowing our neighbors, the loyalties of place have broken down, and our associations are stretched over large territories, cemented by very little direct contact. ... And so you find an

overwhelming demand upon the press for human interest stories, for personal details opened to the vast public. Gossip is organized and we do by telegraph what was done in the village store.

"Even lust," he remarked, "has become elaborate and secondhand."

Most importantly, Lippmann's discovery of distension, like his earlier unwrapping of unreason, is viewed as a lever for improvement. When all was said and done, the fading role of old-fashioned public consent was not a cause for despair. Public apathy and ignorance were cancers in American politics. But if science can analyze these conditions, then it could surely master them.

Lippmann abandoned socialism in 1912 because it relied too heavily on what turned out to be "half-baked people", products of "the unwatered hinterland of the citizen." Lest there be any doubt about the matter, he introduced *Drift and Mastery* with these words: "if the younger critics are to meet the issues of their generation, they must give their attention, not so much to the evils of authority, as to the weaknesses of democracy."

The great danger, as he saw it, was that, like sex for the Victorians, the true powers of unreason and distension would be misunderstood, minimized, and even repressed, to the point that they would undermine both mental and social order. But if leaders could account for the irrational, then they could also harness it. If they could acknowledge the steady "blotting out [of] village culture," then they might find remedies in "the infusion of scientific method, the careful application of administrative techniques, the organization and education of the consumer for control."

NEW POTENTIALS AND NEW HAZARDS

Even as Lippmann moved comfortably to the language of social control, he saw increasing potential in the orchestration of public language.

In *A Preface to Politics*, he cited the "publicity agent" as an example of what good leadership must accomplish and brashly suggests that even "the vile practice of yellow newspapers and chauvinistic politicians" could be a potential model. He seems, at times, to savor references that would stun his audience.

> Religion, patriotism, race, and sex are the favorite red herrings of foul political method—they are the most successful because they explode so easily and flood the mind with those unconscious prejudices which make critical thinking difficult. Yet for all its abuse, the deliberate choice of issues is one of the high selective arts of the statesman. In the debased form we know it there is little encouragement. But the devil is merely a fallen angel, and when God lost Satan he lost one of his best lieutenants. It is always a pretty good working rule that whatever is a great power of evil may become a great power for good.

Lippmann thus announced a hopeful anthem for a new scientific age. He forthrightly endorsed "the importance of style, propaganda, the popularization of ideas." Successful politicians, he pointed out, campaign for office not with syllogisms but with slogans. Public rhetoric must "energize politics" and "harness blind impulses to particular purposes." This process would require, he suggested, the adaptability of the advertiser, the journalist, the vaudevillian, and even someone like P.T. Barnum. All of these people, he submitted, have observed "the psychology of the Golden Rule," an awareness of how the needs of others resemble one's own. Popular whims and fads, from the World Series to cheap novels, are the stuff of which strong leaders build great movements. Only superficial people dislike the superficial, he said, quoting Oscar Wilde.

"In actual life, yes, in the moil and toil of propaganda, movements, causes, and agitations, the statesman-inventors and the political psychologists find material for their work." His advice resembles that of a later writer, Joan Didion, when she advised an audience of graduating students to "just live in the mess."

Lippmann drove the point home by invoking the teachings of Jesus Christ. If, like Jesus, we make human nature the center of our concern, then we can direct enormous reserves of power to glorious ends. "Let the exploration of human need and desire become a deliberate purpose of statecraft," he concluded. Such passages could almost be seen, at points, as predicting Dale Carnegie's advice on *How to Win Friends and Influence People*.

The hero of *A Preface to Politics* was the man who brought publicity to government, Theodore Roosevelt, for whom Lippmann had even done a bit of speechwriting at one point. Lippmann told Roosevelt later that the book "owes a great deal to you." He viewed Roosevelt as "the translator of agitations," a man "in whom millions of people felt the embodiment of their own will." Those who had rejected his leadership were mere "laggards." Did people say that Roosevelt tried to be all things to all men? Well, that was just "a left-handed way of stating a truth. A more generous interpretation would be to say that he had tried to be inclusive, ... to be the leader of factions at war with one another."

Edward Bernays would later make a "segmental approach" to a variegated public a cornerstone of his own methodology. For Walter Lippmann, the successful application of segmental strategies by the president of his younger years qualified Roosevelt as a "political genius" who "haunts political thinking." He concluded, "I believe we need offer no apologies for making Mr. Roosevelt stand as the working model for a possible American statesman at the beginning of the Twentieth Century."

To be sure, there was a clear downside risk in the new power of public language. Freud had shown how the mind invests words with emotional significance, how it "cloaks a deep meaning in a shallow incident. ... Words, theories, symbols, slogans, abstractions of all kinds are nothing but the porous vessels into which life flows, is contained for a time, and then passes through." Improperly used, symbols can be mere "shadows of events," a screen or even a "Chinese Wall" that "cuts us off from the culture of the world." Lippmann's analysis anticipated the famous argument of his later book, *Public Opinion*, where he posited the role of "stereotypes" in shaping human thought.

But if there was a downside risk to symbolic language, there was also an upside opportunity. In making that point initially in *Preface to Politics*, Lippmann drew heavily on the work of Freud, James, Machiavelli, Nietzsche, and most significantly, the French syndicalist Georges Sorel. He was particularly impressed by Sorel's argument that the socially useful symbol, which he called the myth, must be judged by its instrumental effectiveness and not by its descriptive accuracy. It is designed to rally emotions rather than to explain ideas.

But what to do about those who would misuse such skills? If the devil's techniques could be appropriated for noble purposes, then what was to prevent the devil from reclaiming them for his own ends? Such questions were in Charles Forcey's mind when he worried that Lippmann had been sanctioning leadership by "calculated deceit if necessary."

In *Drift and Mastery* a year later, Lippmann presented the matter less cynically and more carefully. He favored terms like *education*, *discipline*, and *science* in describing the instruments of leadership, but he still maintained that "visions," "dreams," and "passionate ideas" should be part of mastery's arsenal.

A new class of scientific business managers ("industrial statesmen") was lauded; so were the labor leader, the head of the consumer cooperative, the efficiency engineer, the conservationist, and the teacher. The government administrator with scientific training joined the orating Roosevelt as "the genius among politicians." The tool of choice was that of sensible public information, distributed through artful publicity.

The need for such redeeming tools was becoming ever more urgent. Consumers could, after all, become "a fickle and superstitious mob, incapable of any real judgment as to what it wants or how it is to get what it thinks it would like." The mounting problem was exemplified by bewildering, garish advertising, a "deceptive clamor that disfigures the scenery, covers fences, plasters the city, and blinks and winks at you through the night." Abusive publicity had become a metaphor for modern civilization:

> the eastern sky ablaze with chewing gum, the northern with tooth-brushes and underwear, the western with whiskey, and the southern with petticoats, the whole heavens brilliant with monstrously flirtatious women, ... a rivulet of [magazine] text trickling through meadows of automobiles, baking powders, corsets and kodaks.

The resulting disorientation has made us all into spiritual immigrants, Lippmann continued, suffering from a "scattering of soul." His own emotion rising, he continued to focus on discombobulating symbols. His language still resonates.

> The modern man is not yet settled in his world. It is strange to him, terrifying, alluring, and incomprehensibly big. The evidence is every-where: the amusements of the city; the jokes that pass for jokes; the

blare that stands for beauty, the folksongs of Broadway, the feeble and apologetic pulpits, the cruel standards of success, raucous purity. We make love to ragtime and we die to it. We are blown hither and thither like litter before the wind. ...

Our days are lumps of undigested experience. You have only to study what newspapers regard as news to see how we are torn and twisted by the irrelevant: in frenzy about issues that do not concern us, bored with those that do. Is it a wild mistake to say that the absence of central authority has disorganized our souls, that our souls are like Peer Gynt's onion, in that they lack a kernel?

The organizing kernel, the "central authority," must, of course, be the expert leader. A public that cannot protect itself must rely on "experts backed with authority to enforce their decisions." The experts, in turn, must compete with the advertiser for the ear and eye of the consumer; they must learn to "drown out raucous ragtime."

SCIENCE AS THE DISCIPLINE OF DEMOCRACY

Lippmann's objective throughout this period was not to forsake democracy but to save it. Ronald Steel summed it up well: "Democracy must be protected from the masses." Or as others suggested, the "people" must be protected from the "crowd."

A lingering respect for democratic input was evident when Lippmann cited a comment from *La Follette's Magazine* that "the composite judgment is always safer and wiser and stronger and more unselfish than the judgment of any one individual mind." But he disagreed with the editors' view that elite plutocrats were the primary problem. To the contrary, only "administrative power" could make democracy work. In a late chapter of *Drift and Mastery* called "Modern Communion," the author again invoked the potential of science:

For the discipline of science is the only one which gives any assurance that from the same set of facts men will come approximately to the same conclusion. And as the modern world can be civilized only by the effort of innumerable people, we have a right to call science the discipline of democracy. ... Mastery is inevitably a matter of cooperation, which means that a great variety of people working in different ways must find some order in their specialties.

"Order in their specialties" is a phrase that reflects a respect for an idealized public that was never fully absent from Lippmann's thought. Steel would describe such exceptional moments as ones in which Lippmann would reveal a certain "vulnerability and romanticism."

Significantly, Lippmann now posits a Wilsonian notion of two publics, distinguishing between "public opinion" on the one hand and "the will of the people" on the other. The first, he said, was expressed in editorials, speeches, and headlines; it was superficial and inconstant, a product of the "masses," the "crowd." The second was deeply rooted in the local life of the people and their long-established habits. What had gone wrong, he feared, was "that American opinion has become less and less representative of American intentions." On behalf of American intentions, leaders like Wilson should reshape American opinion.

But even this guarded faith in an amorphous public would fade considerably by the time *Public Opinion* was published in 1922. It was nearly invisible when *The Phantom Public* came out in 1925. It would make a comeback of sorts in *A Preface to Morals* in 1929, and it would ascend, potentially and theoretically, to a still higher place in Lippmann's *The Good Society* of 1935 and *The Public Philosophy* twenty additional years later. In these later works, participation by an enlightened public, faithful to civil norms, would be seen as an ideal offset to the excesses of centralized control. But in most of his writings, early and later, it was the rational leader who saved the ill-informed public.

"SOMETHING HAD GONE BADLY WRONG"

When Lippmann returned from Paris in early 1919, he felt, as Arthur Schlesinger Jr. has written, "that something had gone badly wrong, that his work had miscarried." In a long article called "Unrest," which ran in the *New Republic* in November 1919, he reiterated earlier themes: the danger of drift and the use of public information to stabilize the public mind. But his emphasis had begun to shift. It was not information itself but the *quality* of that information that now became his central focus. Disorienting information was now the unmistakable villain. The troubles abroad and at home in 1919, he suggested, resulted from the fact that even leading citizens had been "saturated with propaganda." Half believing everything, they actually believed nothing. Order, stability, and control now depended less on rallying emotions than on "disentangling" them.

> A time when all information is what the Europeans call tendentious, when the people are alternately let down, frustrated, screwed up, frustrated, and let down, is one in which realistic judgment is difficult. ... And thus the nation finds itself, in the face of aggravated problems, without any source of information that it can really trust and without leaders to interpret events. ... The one thing, the only thing that could stabilize men's mind in the gigantic flux and shift of the present world is trustworthy news, unadulterated data, fair reporting, disinterested fact. "Your eyes were unlidded, your ears were unstopped."

The unlidding of eyes and the unstopping of ears was still presented in this article as something that is done for the public and not by them. Once this clarifying process has been accomplished, then public opinion can perhaps be restored to philosophical favor. And if that happens, then we might dare to believe again "that somehow it represents the disinterested thought of the community."

> The idea of a Public is simply a short way of expressing the great faith
> that a group of men and women will always disentangle themselves
> from their prejudices and will be sufficiently powerful to summon the
> partisans before the bar of reason; and that evidence, not mere jaw,
> will then decide.

He ended on a Wilsonian note: "For a reduction of this panic my own hopes are in what might be called the latent public. ... They are there. They can be summoned."

But even these hopeful words about a latent public were not unqualified. This immediate postwar appraisal reflected the writer's doubts when it candidly suggested that an ideal, disinterested public is such an attractive idea that "if it did not exist we should have to invent it." Without such a hope, our social life becomes "sheer commotion," Lippmann realized. The news systems of the world, sadly, make it possible "to fool most of the Public a good part of the time." To have confidence in even some latent public is merely "a faith," a "precious ideal," a loyalty that can comfort us "in the lean and bitter time which may be ahead."

Perhaps for those whose faith is fierce enough, the public might still reign symbolically, a constitutional monarch in the kingdom it once ruled. The latent public and the controlling expert are scientific partners, but the public is still latent, and the expert still controls.

John Dewey's similar reconciliation flowed out of a rigorous dialectical commitment. Lippmann's dualism seems to result from the fact that he, quite realistically, wanted to have things both ways.

His article on "Unrest" was paralleled by two other 1919 essays in the *Atlantic Monthly*, published together in book form under the title *Liberty and News* in 1920. Things were getting worse. The Great Society was now even more scattered and disorganized. Public communication had broken down; "in an exact sense the present crisis of western democracy is a crisis in journalism." This was not the fault of immoral newspapers, but rather "the intricate result of a civilization too extensive for any man's personal observation." The result had been "an incredible medley of fact, propaganda, rumor, suspicion, clues, hopes and fears." Perhaps the expert journalist could still save the people from these threats, but that would depend on journalists recognizing that they held "one of the truly sacred and priestly offices in a democracy."

Journalism's legitimizing mandate might seem, in this telling, to have a mysterious aspect; it was "sacred" and "priestly." But the all-important task of the newly professional journalist was to bring more science into journalism. Its training schools must be improved, its skills upgraded. Journalists must seek the help of research institutes and information agencies. Other proposals included an international news agency, new controls on publishers, and requirements for divulging sources of information. In the best of all worlds, a court might be established in which misleading propagandists could be brought to trial—anticipating a broad array of proposals for responsible regulation of media, including social media, in more recent years.

If Lippmann was briefly hopeful about journalism's prospects in the fall of 1919, by the next summer he had become less confident. With Charles Merz, a noted New York editor who had served with him in his wartime propaganda mission, he published in the *New Republic* an extensive and devastating critique of stories that the *New York Times* had carried on the Russian Revolution over a three-year period. The coverage had been "a disaster," the two critics convincingly concluded. Their mood was expressed perfectly in the quotation from *The Iliad* that prefaced the important article.

> Enlighten me now, O Muses, tenants of Olympian homes,
>
> For you are goddesses, inside on everything, know everything.
>
> But we mortals hear only the news, and know nothing at all.

FROM SKEPTICISM TO CYNICISM

For Lippmann and for his generation, long-brewing skepticism was fast turning to cynicism. The antiradical Red Scare of 1919 and 1920 contributed further to that process. But one more heavy straw was added to the camel's back during these same months. For those who had hoped, through everything, that a Roosevelt or Wilson could again speak for a wiser, latent public, the nomination and subsequent election of Warren Harding to the US presidency in November of 1920 was a profoundly discouraging blow. It mocked that credulous identification of leader and public that had been a keystone of Progressive optimism.

Lippmann vented his immediate reaction in an article adroitly entitled "The Crude Barbarian and the Noble Savage." Disturbed, too, by D.H. Lawrence's recent romanticizing of American innocents, he complained about "a public opinion that quakes before the word highbrow as if it denoted a secret sin." He listed as evidence of public crudity the fact that they "have just overwhelmingly elected a President who took pains to put himself on record against excellence."

It was all too much. In March 1921 the *New Republic* announced Lippmann's departure from his editorial position. He retreated to a new country home in Wading River, New York, on Long Island Sound, to write a book he had been contemplating for some time. Since 1913 he had contended that someone should sit down and explain analytically what the crowd psychologists explained metaphorically. He had repeated the suggestion in reviews of crowd psychology studies whenever they appeared. He recognized that those who wrote about such things were putting their finger on "the greatest weakness of popular government," but unfortunately most of them were "too much diverted by [the] Group Mind to write a book about minds in a group." He was appalled, he had written in *Liberty and the News*, that there was "not one, single, significant study of the process of public opinion."

Sidney Brooks had made the same complaint in the *North American Review* in 1914: "Where is the philosopher who will write about this strange force ... furnishing the world with a new set of nerves ... this ubiquitous phenomenon of publicity?" In 1922 Brooks received his answer when Walter Lippmann published *Public Opinion*, still puzzling, even in its pages, that he was the first to give serious, sustained attention to the topic.

"THE MOST EFFECTIVE INDICTMENT OF DEMOCRACY"

Historian Arthur Schlesinger Jr. shared this appraisal of *Public Opinion* in 1959, thirty-seven years after its appearance: "The stupefying mass of writing, both learned and popular, which has appeared on this subject in the last quarter-century has added surprisingly little to Lippmann's analysis." Even today, six additional decades after Schlesinger's comment, the book is still regarded as a landmark work in the canon of political philosophy, one that still appears on reading lists across the academic world.

Its import had been quickly recognized. The *New Republic*, which had serialized part of the book, carried a review in May 1922 that made readers take sharp notice. This book, it began, is "so readable, its manner so brilliant, that one almost forgets that it is ... perhaps the most effective indictment of democracy as currently conceived ever penned." Such superlative comments might have seemed a bit overstated if had they not come from one of the handful of Americans best qualified to make such a judgment. That reviewer was John Dewey.

Dewey's own hopes for "scientific democracy" had paralleled Lippmann's, and the latter's loss of faith shook Dewey's world as well. He could not say enough about what the analysis meant for him. It was

> a more significant statement of the genuine "problem of knowledge" than professional epistemological philosophers have managed to give. ... It shivers most of our illusions, and this particular Humpty Dumpty can never be put together again for anyone who reads these chapters with an open mind. ... Mr. Lippmann has thrown into clearer relief than any other writer the fundamental difficulty of democracy.

The book drew, of course, on insights that others had shared earlier. A leading argument of the book was about public dependence on "pictures in our heads," creating a "pseudo-environment" that made it almost impossible for people "to see the world steadily and see it whole." In presenting the term *stereotypes*, Lippmann found a fresh way to discuss an idea that was at least somewhat familiar to readers of Cooley or Wallas, of James or Bergson or Sorel. Indeed, it was extremely familiar to John Dewey, whose own book, *How We Think*, was also quoted in *Public Opinion* to illustrate the concept.

Lippmann himself had touched on the topic, if not the precise language, in 1913. Words are inflexible vessels, he had posited. "And when life's expansion demands some new container, nothing is more difficult than the realization that the old vessels cannot be stretched to the present need."

"Because of its power to siphon emotion out of distinct ideas," he continued in 1922, "the symbol is both a mechanism of solidarity and a mechanism of exploitation." When people are in a hurry and it is "more important to act than to understand," then "the manipulation of masses through symbols may be the only quick way of having a critical thing done." He acknowledged that "the abandonment of all stereotypes for a wholly innocent approach to experience would impoverish human life." He cited Alexander Hamilton and Charles Evans Hughes as leaders who had utilized "a hierarchy of symbols" for the purpose of "crystallizing a common will."

Lippmann's 1922 discussion of the press, highlighting inevitable journalistic failures, echoed that of *Liberty and the News*. But it went a good deal further. Overweening complexity made reporting unmanageable; a new sense of remoteness made it unreliable. Events were reported not because of their intrinsic importance but because someone had "made an issue" out of them. Upton Sinclair's *The Brass Check* was wrong to blame these failures on moral failure or economic causes. As Lincoln Steffens said, the problem was usually not one of morality but of "anatomy." Part of the cure was to find ways to update and improve reporting. Lippmann made some additional suggestions for employing independent expertise, but the scale of the challenge seemed overwhelming.

Lippmann's conclusions marked a hyper-realistic plunge into political processes that seemed to parallel the myth-destroying work of Machiavelli—and even the clear-eyed critiques of Aristotle. He summed up his case in sentences designed to stun the tender minded: "The Court of Public Opinion, open day and night, is to lay down the law for everything all the time. It is not workable. And when you consider the nature of news, it is not even thinkable." The will of the people had been replaced, he said, by "the manufacture of consent."

> And so ... the practice of democracy has turned a corner. A revolution is taking place, infinitely more significant than any shifting of economic power. ... Within the life of the generation now in control of affairs, persuasion has become a self-conscious art ... it is no daring prophecy to say that the knowledge of how to create consent will alter every political calculation and modify every political premise. It is no longer possible to believe in the original dogma of democracy, that the knowledge of human affairs comes up spontaneously from the human heart.

It was a painful description. And still a highly relevant one.

It was not an entirely new judgment. But why then did John Dewey find the book so newly compelling? Why did Lippmann feel that it represented a turning point in his own thinking? The answer was the opposite of what some readers were inferring. The great new problem was the realization that even expert, scientific leaders could NOT, in fact, subject popular sentiment to their intelligent control, at least not on a reliable basis.

What propaganda meant for Lippmann was not so much the threat of excessive control but the dangers of no control. His concern as early as 1913 had not been with manipulative advocates but with "deceptive clamor," the environment of jazz and ragtime, of blinking lights at night, of news that blows men "hither and thither." He had long been fearful of public panic, instability, inconstancy, superficial impulse, and mob hysteria. Disorganized and undependable information produced a disorganized and undependable public. And it was not clear just what might be done about it.

In *Public Opinion*, disorganization finally got the upper hand. Unreason and distension had become too great. What disturbed Dewey when he reviewed *Public Opinion* was that even well-informed and well-intentioned leadership had failed. The runaway horse of which Lippmann had written in *A Preface to Politics* had thrown its rider of last resort.

The weakness of the new information arena was not illustrated by Wilson's ability to rally the nation to war but by his inability to rally it to the League of Nations. It was not Creel's successes that bothered Lippmann but his failures. The heroic capacities of Roosevelt and Wilson did not cause him to rethink his democratic philosophy; the mediocrity of Harding did.

The failure of effective leaders, of course, opened the way for demagogues who could take advantage of the chaos. Plato had seen it all coming, warning that "hyper democracy" would lead to tyrannical evils. Lippmann speaks tellingly about how self-serving, conscience-less propagandists could exploit the confusion, dancing agilely upon the mad surface of opinion.

Could more expert leaders still fight them off? For Lippmann, the evidence was not encouraging. The "unconscious constellations of feeling" that produce stereotypes had turned insurgent and insubordinate. Runaway stereotypes had so thoroughly subjectivized meaning that constructive discourse was nearly impossible; "the identical story is not the same story to all who hear it." Each playgoer writes himself into the drama, creates his own separate script, and "as the audience grows larger, the number of common words diminishes." While later philosophers might write hopefully about embracing "pluralism," Lippmann was realistically transfixed by fragmentation. And, indeed, by polarization.

How could even the best scientist organize and control such a world? "Psychology indicates how essentially casual is the nexus between the particular stimulus and the particular response." Or as Lasswell would later say, symbols were merely "chips in the baccarat of catharsis and readjustment."

The problem was not simply that people lived in a pseudo-environment but that everybody's pseudo-environment was different. While people may "live in the same world ... they think and feel in different ones." Even when they do the same things, they do them for different reasons. Lippmann cited G.K. Chesterton's view that to expect organized social reactions is to base our hopes not "on a communion, or even on a convention, but rather on a coincidence."

Lippmann sealed the point by citing not only the variety of individual mentalities at work in the Great Society but also the variety of "governments, the parties, the corporations, the societies, the social sets, the trades and professions, universities, sects and nationalities of the world." To expect that social order can be ordained in such circumstances was indeed to count on "coincidence."

Later students of propaganda would pick up on the element of chance in the formulation of public opinion. They would even use it as a calming reminder in the face of panic about demagogic propagandists. The most that the demagogue finally could do, said Leonard Doob in the 1930s, was "to load his gun with buckshot," hoping to strike as many vulnerable souls as possible. Similarly, in 1961 the era's great scholar of public opinion, V.O. Key, would compare the public advocacy process to "dropping a handful of confetti from the rim of the Grand Canyon with the objective of striking a man astride a burro on the canyon floor." But if the dangerous propagandist could not reliably control his targeting (at least before the advent of social media), then could the scientific reformer really do any better?

While the constructive leader could still try to employ myths that might attract a certain following, it was probably safer, Lippmann thought, to drift with superficial tastes than to try to transform them. "The stereotypes can be altered, but not in time to guarantee success when the film is released six months from now." Not only was there no heroic crowd mind; there was not even Tardian imitation. There was usually just confusion. It is no longer the mobilized and purposeful crowd that is to be feared but rather "the trampling and the roar of a bewildered herd."

The Great Society was too extended and diverse to be organized by anyone. Nobody, Lippmann observed, could have tried harder than George Creel to overcome this problem and to "carry quickly a fairly uniform set of ideas to all the people of a nation." In fact, while the war continued, the Wilson administration "very largely succeeded."

> But think of the dogged work, the complicated ingenuity, the money and the personnel that were required. Nothing like that exists in time of peace, and as a corollary there are whole sections, there are vast groups, ghettoes, enclaves and classes that hear only vaguely about much that is going on.

As a result, people "live in grooves ... shut in among their own affairs, barred out of larger affairs, meet few people not of their own sort, read little." They are motivated neither to follow nor to understand critical events. In sum, "the true interests of the people no longer interest the people."

The problem, to be sure, was not that the public was stupid, evil, or ill motivated. These were good people, basically, with their own lives to live, their own families to raise, their own challenges to resolve. It was unrealistic to expect such a public to follow adequately the ins and outs of policy discussions or to sort out the relative merits of disputing assessments—or even to resist emotional appeals to powerful stereotypes. Nor was it any longer realistic to think that heroic communicators could remedy the problem.

The fragments left behind with the coming of the Great Society cannot easily be put back together, he concluded. The sense of a common code is gone, and with it the possibility of deeply shared norms. (He would make this ongoing, elusive quest for publicly accepted civil norms the central theme of his 1955 treatise on *The Public Philosophy*, his last major book, one he said that was nearly two decades in the making.) But the difficulty of the challenge had been set down clearly in 1922. Long before the terms were popularized in twenty-first century analyses, what seemed to be developing in Lippmann's view was indeed a "postfact, posttruth" society.

Though Lippmann did mention again in *Public Opinion* some of the scientific ameliorations he proposed two years earlier in *Liberty and the News*, he explicitly recanted the faint optimism of that book. He did not then fully understand, he allowed, what he now called his "most fertile" hypothesis: "that news and truth are not the same thing and must be clearly distinguished." It remains a striking insight a century later. "Society is so suffused with subjectivity" that even the expert journalist has become its victim. Censorship, obscurity, and complexity are more than even the best reporters can handle.

The disjunction was complete. News, like myth, cannot be tested objectively. Homer's words are no longer hyperbole: "But we mortals hear only the news, and know nothing at all." As the popular fictional bartender Mr. Dooley put it in one of Finley Peter Dunne's columns, "sin is news and news is sin."

Stretched too far by modern civilization, the strings between leader and public had snapped. Neither old-fashioned notions of public sovereignty nor new visions about scientific democracy seemed able to restore it. What then are we left with? George Sylvester Viereck summed up the temper of the age in introducing his 1930 book *Spreading Germs of Hate*:

> I fought for what I deemed the right / I saw the Truth, I was her knight.
>
> My foeman, too, were thus aflame, / Blind chessmen in the obscure game
>
> Of some malign divinity. / Now with unfolding eyes we see
>
> The paradox of every fight, / That both are wrong and both are right,
>
> That friend is foe and foe is friend / And nothing matters in the end.

WHEN NOTHING MATTERS: THE ONGOING SEARCH

"Nothing matters anymore," was to become a trope for *Saturday Night Live's* satirical television assessment of the information climate in the months following the 2016 US elections. Whether thoughtful words can really "matter" again remains, of course, a disturbing question. It was for Lippmann, too. His own critique of public opinion was devastating, but he felt obliged to continue the search at least for partial remedies.

In the first place, there might still be a way in which the public might be taught to examine symbols, question sources, and boil "the fat" out of their stereotypes. The process, resembling psychoanalysis, might be painful at first, but it can bring "an immense relief and a pride" when people learn to see themselves honestly. "The scene turns vivid and full," Lippmann posited, once the public's latent emotional energy can be reattached to a "hearty appreciation of scientific method."

What was needed, he said as he searched for answers, was a public "Socrates" who would cross-examine the careless use of words. Could the public perhaps be taught to say "that labor groups C and M, but not X, are underpaid, instead of saying that Labor is Exploited?" Sometimes "the snarl is too huge and ancient for quick unsnarling. Sometimes … there are layers upon layers of memory reaching back to infancy, which have to be separated and named." But perhaps "re-education" might eventually reobjectify language so that "public opinion in the eulogistic sense of the term can exist."

In addition, Lippmann still treasured a slim hope that better management of information, realized through reformed journalism and a network of data-gathering intelligence bureaus, could reintegrate the Great Society. Like his earlier suggestions in this regard, this part of the book was greeted most skeptically—given the daunting message that had preceded it. Nonetheless, Lippmann still could not give up on the possibility "that unseen environments can be reported effectively to divergent groups of people." It would be difficult, "but now there is a way out, a long one to be sure, but a way. It is fundamentally the same way as that which has enabled a citizen of Chicago, with no better eyes or ears than an Athenian, to see and hear over great distances."

Humanity might eventually learn to deal reasonably with an unreasonable world, but only "over a long run of time." The world moves too fast for the current capacities of scientific journalism. It may be, as Sophocles said, that a lie never lives to be old, Lippmann recognized.   But he then also cited the words of Mark Sullivan who claimed that for a wartime atrocity story to live even briefly was "as regards effect, to live forever." A leading American journalist, William Allen White, underscored the point: "I think on the whole, sooner later, the American people do get the truth. But they often get it when it is cold potatoes and does them no good."

Whatever his long-run dreams, Lippmann's immediate advice reflected his realistic instincts. Perhaps there were certain broad questions on which the public could still comment, "essentially principles of procedure," but on the whole, public opinion should be treated as one would treat an "outsider." The governing process was the province of the elite. It was for their benefit that a new intelligence machinery should be set up, "a running audit which makes work intelligible to those who do it."

Like the parable of Plato's Cave with which he had opened *Public Opinion*, demonstrating the shadowy nature of the pseudo-environment, the illustration that ended the book came from Plato's *Republic*. "Until philosophers are kings," Socrates had there observed, "cities will never cease from ill—no, nor the human race." In his less noted series of lectures at the University of Virginia in 1927, Lippmann would share his view that it was actually democracy in the end which had been responsible for Socrates' death. Little wonder then that Plato and Socrates had dreamed about a day when philosophers would be the kings. And yet, as Lippmann interprets the *Republic* account in the closing pages of *Public Opinion*, Socrates comes quickly to see the futility of this romantic possibility and then simply ends the discussion.

Lippmann goes to analyze this outcome. For Socrates (and Plato), he suggests, the fault lay not with the philosophers of the day but with "those who will not use them." And yet, Lippmann then argues, "The pilot of an imperiled ship should not humbly beg the sailors to be commanded by him—that is not the order of nature." To expect the public to step up and save the day is simply unrealistic. And so it is that Lippmann concludes in no uncertain terms that that Plato had simply ended the Socrates story too early. He had cut Socrates off rather than enabling him to grapple further with the issue. "And with this haughty gesture," as Lippmann tellingly describes Socrates departure, "he hurriedly picked up the tools of reason, and disappeared into the Academy, leaving the world to Machiavelli."

Walter Lippmann was determined not to "disappear into the Academy"—and he was even more determined not to "give up the tools of reason." Yes, down through the centuries of combat between reason and politics, a good many champions of reason had chosen, like Socrates, to outline a hopeful nirvana and then retire from the struggle. But not Lippmann. The fact is, he said, that "the ship is at sea" with mutineers on board (the public), and a good, responsible pilot could not respond to the mutiny by simply saying "so much the worse for us all." Nor would the good pilot be able to find time during the mutiny to educate each sailor to respect the pilot's expertise. Education is a matter of years, the emergency a matter of hours. "In the crisis, the only advice is to use a gun, or make a speech, utter a stirring slogan, offer a compromise, employ any quick means available to quell the mutiny."

This, then, was the state of public opinion as Walter Lippmann understood it in the 1920s, a potentially mutinous force threatening peril to the ship of state. The myth, the slogan, if they cannot be used to rally mass opinion, could at least help quell the mutiny.

Lippmann had written in *A Preface to Politics* that poor leaders were faced the wrong way on a runaway horse; good leadership meant turning around so that one might direct and control the animal. Now that he saw how the horse really behaves, repeatedly throwing the best of riders, his advice was no longer to try to bridle the beast but at least, perhaps, to corral it.

CONTINUING INFLUENCE

The themes enunciated in *Public Opinion* triggered a host of notable responses. More and better public information, for example, quickly became the central concern of the powerful consumer's movement. The book also heralded a new movement to develop the field of professional journalism—including the launch of important university journalism schools. It spurred calls for a dedicated Labor or Reform press, as well as idealistic experiments in educational broadcasting. Harold Lasswell's vigorous promotion of such possibilities, including the role of educational film, caused one of his students to remark, "Evidently the world can be saved if man can stand the eyestrain."

John Dewey picked up on Lippmann's discussion of transcending myths in his major book, *The Public and Its Problems,* in 1927. Philosophers like Sidney Hook and Max Lerner also embraced the instrumental use of social symbolism. It was in that same spirit that the influential Washington lawyer Thurman Arnold called prominently in the mid-1930s for more intelligent "control over our ceremonies and creeds." His advice was taken. The *Washington Post*'s art and architecture critic, Phillip Kennicott, recalled the effort with some dismay in 2016. "As the great American family grew more ambitious, fractious and diffuse, and felt threatened on all sides in the 1920s and 1930s, its need for shrines was so powerful that it didn't bother with history or authenticity." Nor has the debate over public shrines since subsided.

At the same time, Lippmann's hopes for a more discerning use of language were widely echoed as his book was more widely read. Educators arranged curricula that would teach children to mistrust what they normally read, to reach what Lasswell called the "aha!" level of sophistication. Children must learn, Dorothy Thompson added, to say "Yeah?" instead of "Yea, Lord!" Later generations would similarly seek an answer in "media literacy."

The ambitious Institute for Propaganda Analysis (IPA) would propose an elaborate, related technique: an intricate series of symbols for marking in the margin of a book or newspaper the "glittering generality," the "band-wagon" appeal, the use of "card stacking" or "plain folks," or other rhetorical strategies. One enterprising student dramatized the futility of this process by carefully marking in the margin of the IPA's own fulsome explanation of its system the same symbols, denoting the same logical fallacies. The IPA would soon disappear, seen by many as a partisan propaganda vehicle in its own right.

Perhaps the most notable opposition to misleading language came from the movement for semantic purity, including advocates for positivist philosophy as well as for realist literature. Bertrand Russell was one such voice (he once wanted to simply "outlaw propaganda"). Ernest Hemingway was another. The latter's attack on linguistic abstraction was captured in a famous passage from *A Farewell to Arms:*

> I was always embarrassed by the words sacred, glorious, and sacrifice and the expression in vain. ... There were many words that you could not stand to hear and finally only the names of places had dignity.

Certain numbers were the same way and certain dates and these with the names of the places were all you could say and have them mean anything.

In *The Tyranny of Words* in 1935, Stuart Chase joined the attack on

> mystics, spellbinders, theologians, spiritualists, Herr Goebbels, the pain and beauty advertisers, the formal logicians, the backers of the tortoise against Achilles. Around the fact the fakers throw their verbal smoke. But ultimately the fog lifts. It must lift. … We cannot live on lies, fantasies and propaganda.

Stuart Chase's book—and the plain speech movement in which it played a prominent role—drew heavily on the penetrating work of the British philosophers C.K. Ogden and I.A. Richards. Like other linguistic positivists, they rejected the abstract, the insubstantial, and the introspective. Their landmark book, *The Meaning of Meaning*, was published in 1923, just after *Public Opinion*, building on the theories of the Swiss semiologist Ferdinand de Saussure.

Forty years later, a different sort of nominalist, the University of Chicago professor Daniel Boorstin, published *The Image: A Guide to Pseudo-events in America.* It was an iconoclastic work in the fullest sense of that term, rebelling against all unnatural representations of reality, from the televised political convention to the often manipulated *Congressional Record.* Boorstin, too, cited the influence of Lippmann's study.

In 1925 Lippmann published a follow-up work called *The Phantom Public*, qualifying even some of the possibilities that he had suggested earlier. More sufficient education? Not likely: "The problems of the modern world appear and change faster than any set of teachers can grasp them." He compared the public to the spectator in the last row of the theater, who must always "arrive in the middle of the third act and will leave before the last curtain … identifying the villain and hero and no more." But again, this was not so much a reflection on human intelligence as a description of the new information world.

At best, in such a world, the public might still work to protect just one remaining interest: "that all special interests shall act according to settled rule … to support the ins when things are going well; to support the outs when they seem to be going badly, this … is the essence of popular government."

Expecting too much of the voter was to raise a false ideal. "I do not mean an undesirable ideal. I mean an unattainable ideal, bad only in the sense that it is bad for a fat man to try to be a ballet dancer. … The ideal of the omni-competent, sovereign citizen is, in my opinion, such a false ideal. It is unattainable. The pursuit of it is misleading. The failure to achieve it has produced the current disenchantment."

With Freud (who took the words from Milton), Lippmann now sought "what reinforcement we may gain from hope; if not, what resolution from despair." That realistic tone would dominate his *Preface to Morals* of 1929 and, in 1937, *The Good Society*.

The latter book would call for a determined decentralization of government. It was a step that brought him full cycle, back to a world before the advent of the Great Society. Given the impossibility of achieving a coherent global village, he now looked to the older, local village as a possible savior, reflecting Aristotle's sense that the face-to-face arena might best nourish true democracy. (The approach has gained very recent reinforcement on many fronts; in the hopeful locality-by-locality reportage of James and Deborah Fallows, for example, as well the close attention of writers like Benjamin Barber and Neal Peirce.)

Many of Lippmann's associates had long been pressing the localism theme. Graham Wallas had idealized the Norwegian towns and villages ... "where everyone seemed to respect themselves." The group discussion movement similarly sought to create small. integral neighborhoods as a way to honor both participation and intelligence. And it was the child of rural Vermont, John Dewey, who concluded his *The Public and Its Problems* with this affirmation:

> Democracy must begin at home, and its home is the neighborly community ... the family, the church, the neighborhood. ... The problem of securing diffused and seminal intelligence can be solved only in the degree in which local communal life becomes a reality. ... The winged words of conversation in immediate intercourse have a vital import lacking in the fixed and frozen words of written speech.

Dewey here identified his passion for the local with a yearning for oral interchange, as opposed to "the fixed and frozen words of written speech." He echoed the dismay of Socrates when he worried about how the invention of the Greek alphabet and the advent of a technology called writing had threatened the rich oral culture of ancient Greece.

Writers about abstract concepts (such as public opinion) are undoubtedly influenced by their own stereotypes as to the how such opinion might be formed. Cooley thought of the newspapers rivaling conversation at breakfast. Dewey returned to the Vermont village. Woodrow Wilson invoked the small towns of the South and West. So did Ivy Lee and George Creel, born a year apart to Confederate families in the rural South.

On the other hand, when Walter Lippmann, like Edward Bernays, thought about "public opinion," he most probably thought of strap hangers on crowded streetcars reading yellow newspapers in the New York City of his boyhood. By such considerations, among others, are intellectual and political history shaped.

* * *

Lipmann knew that his suggestions for helping advance the cause of reason in an anarchic information world were not miracle cures. Even today, many readers still find

Lippmann's unsparing diagnosis more powerful than his potential cures. And yet Lippmann refused to give up on the matter and "leave the world to Machiavelli." Much like the earnest Harvard undergraduate he had once been, he was still disposed to soldier on and to "thank with brief thanksgiving, whatever gods may be."

And so it was that he named the last chapter of *Public Opinion* "An Appeal to Reason." He outlined what he called the seven deadly sins against public reason: hatred, intolerance, suspicion, bigotry, secrecy, fear, and lying. And he concluded, on the final page of his masterwork, with deeply felt words of reassurance that still speak with particular eloquence to later generations who want to believe that something "matters in the end."

> We can do this [the work of reason] all the better if we do not allow frightfulness and fanaticism to impress us so deeply that we throw up our hands peevishly, and lose interest in the longer run of time because we have lost faith in the future of man. There is no ground for this despair, because all the ifs on which ... our destiny hangs, are as pregnant as they ever were. ... It was only Berlin, Moscow, Versailles in 1914 to 1919, not Armageddon ... it is not foolish for men to believe that because another great war took place, that intelligence, courage and effort cannot ever contrive a good life for all men.

Taking stock of his own earlier despair, he found reasons for persistent faith. "Great as was the horror it was not universal. There were corrupt, and there were incorruptible. There were muddles and there were miracles. There was huge lying. There were men with the will to uncover it."

Most importantly, there was the future.

> You can despair of what has never been. But you cannot despair of the possibilities that could exist by virtue of any human quality which a human being has exhibited. And if amidst all the evils of this decade, you have not seen men and women, known moments that you would like to multiply, the Lord himself cannot help you.

Source Notes

PREFACE

Recent histories that have informed this discussion include David Greenberg, *Republic of Spin* (New York, 2016); David M. Kennedy, *Over Here: The First World War and American Society* (Oxford, 1980, 25th anniversary edition, New York, 2004); and Niall Ferguson, *The Square and the Tower* (New York, 2018), esp. p. 406ff.

CHAPTER 1. OLD REALITIES AND NEW PERCEPTIONS

pp. 1.

Edmund Morris, *The Rise of Theodore Roosevelt* (New York, 1979), pp. 658–59 passim. On the filming of Spanish-American War scenes, see, among others: David Greenberg, *Republic of Spin*, pp. 13–16; M. Paul Hoslinger, *War and Popular American Culture* (Westport, CT, 1999), pp. 182–83; and Charles Musser, "The American Vitograph, 1897–1901" in *Film Before Griffith*, ed. John Bell (Berkeley, 1983), pp. 22–66. On Theodore Roosevelt and muckraking, a compelling overview is Doris Kearns Goodwin, *The Bully Pulpit: Theodore Roosevelt, William Howard Taft, and the Golden Age of Journalism* (New York, 2013).

pp. 2.

Thomas Friedman, *The Lexus and the Olive Tree* (New York, 2000), p. xvi; Robert J. Gordon, *The Rise and Fall of American Growth: The U.S. Standard of Living Since the Civil War* (Princeton, NJ, 2016), Part I. *Niall Ferguson in The Square and the Tower* also documents vividly the impact of such changes (including national postal systems), pp. 159–60. The reference to an early mention of the term Fake News comes from an interview with Michelle Nickerson of Loyola University, Chicago, October 6, 2020, on the Professor Buzzkill History Podcast "*Fake News in American History*."

pp. 3.

Robert Wiebe, *The Search for Order, 1887–1920* (New York, 1967), pp. 44–45, 52; John Dewey, *Individualism Old and New* (New York, 1929), pp. 42–43; Harold D. Lasswell, "Propaganda and Mass Insecurity," *Psychiatry* 13 (August 1950): pp. 284–85; W. T. Brande, "Propaganda," in *Dictionary of Science Literature and Art* (London, 1841), quoted in Terence H. Qualter, *Propaganda and Psychological Warfare* (New York, 1962), p. 4.

pp. 4.

Walter Lippmann, *American Inquisitors* (New York, 2017), p. 104. This book republishes a series of lectures which Lippmann gave at the University of Virginia in 1927, perhaps his least familiar publication, but also one of his most insightful.

pp. 5–6.

James Rorty, writing in *Our Master's Voice: Advertising* (New York, 1934), p. 280, anticipated later expressions when he wrote: "Fake, Baloney, Bunk, Apple Sauce, Bull. There are over a hundred slang synonyms for the idea these words express, most of them coined within the last two decades. No other idea has called forth such lavish folk invention." The list today could go on much further, beginning, of course, with the word *spin*. "H. L. Mencken Quotes," BrainyQuote, Xplore Inc., 2018, https://www.brainyquote.com/quotes/h_l_mencken_129257 and 490503.

CHAPTER 2. THE POWER OF SUGGESTION AND THE ECLIPSE OF REASON

pp. 7–10.

Harold D. Lasswell, introduction to *Allied Propaganda and the Collapse of the German Empire in 1918*, by George G. Bruntz, Hoover War Library Publications, No. 13 (Stanford, CA, 1938), pp. v–vi; William James, introduction to *The Psychology of Suggestion: A Research into the Subconscious Nature of Man and Society*, by Boris Sidis (New York, 1898); Harold Stearns, "The Bogey Man," *New Republic* 6 (April 29, 1916): pp. 356–57; Martin Conway, *The Crowd in Peace and War* (New York, 1915); E. L. Godkin, "Panics," an essay of 1873, reprinted in his *Reflections and Comments, 1865–1895* (New York, 1895), p. 79.

pp. 10.

James Harvey Robinson, "Freud Once More," *New Republic* 17 (November 30, 1918): pp. 140–141. See also Lancelot Law Whyte, *The Unconscious Before Freud* (New York, 1960); G. T. W. Patrick, "The Psychology of Crazes," *Popular Science Monthly* 57 (1900): pp. 285–94; G. T. W. Patrick, *The Psychology of Social Reconstruction* (Boston, 1920); Oliver Carlson, *Brisbane: A Candid Biography* (New York, 1937), p. 294; Wilfred Trotter, *The Instinct of the Herd in Peace and War* (London, 1915); William McDougall, *Introduction to Social Psychology* (Boston, 1908); William McDougall, *The Group Mind* (Cambridge, UK, 1920); John Dewey, *Human Nature and Conduct* (New York, 1922); Gustave Le Bon, *The Crowd: A Study of the Popular Mind* (Paris, 1895, with English edition from London, 1896); Gabriel Tarde, *The Law of Imitation* (Paris, 1890), trans. E. E. Parsons (New York, 1903).

pp. 11.

Walter Lippmann, "The Group Mind," *New Republic* 25 (December 15, 1920): pp. 82–86; William McDougall, *The Group Mind*, p. 29; Charles A. Ellwood, "Is Society a Physical Unity? A Rejoinder," *American Journal of Sociology* 10 (March 1905); Harold Stearns, "The Bogey Man," pp. 356–57; Walter Lippmann, "Trotter and Freud," *New Republic* 9 (November 18, 1916): pp. 16–18; Floyd Allport, *Social Psychology* (Boston, 1924), p. 295; Le Bon, *The Crowd*, pp. 182, 32, 9–10, 150, 71.

pp. 12–13.

Sigmund Freud, *Group Psychology and the Analysis of the Ego* (Leipzig, 1921), trans. James Strachey (London, 1922); Philip Rieff, *Freud: The Mind of the Moralist* (New York, 1959), chaps. 6–7; Labert St. Clair, "Keep on a' Courtin' That Girl," *Electric Railway Journal* 60 (September 2, 1922): p. 238; Everett Dean Martin, *The Behavior of Crowds: A Psychological Study* (New York, 1920), pp. 37ff.; Everett Dean Martin, "Some Mechanisms That Distinguish the Crowd from Other Forms of Social Behavior," *Journal of Abnormal and Social Psychology* 18 (1923): pp. 187–205; Walter Lippmann, "Trotter and Freud," p. 16; Wilfred Trotter, *The Instinct of the Herd in Peace and War*, pp. 85, 139ff.; Arthur Christensen, *Politics and Crowd Morality: A Study in the Philosophy of Politics*, trans. Q. Cecil Curtis (London, 1915); Graham Wallas, *Human Nature in Politics*, 2nd ed. (London, 1908), pp. 19, 177; Randolph Bourne, *War and the Intellectuals: Collected Essays, 1915–1919*, ed. Carl Resek, (New York, 1964), pp. 6–14, 69–77, 114, 151.

pp. 14–15.

Robert Darnton, *Mesmerism and the End of the Enlightenment in France* (Cambridge, MA, 1968); J. L. and J.B. Gilder, *Trilbyana: The Rise and Progress of a Popular Novel* (New York, 1895), a short description of the mania, of which 250 copies were published by the editors of the *Critic*. Copy 194 is in the Harvard College Library; George du Maurier, *Trilby* (New York, 1894), pp. 57, 136, 458, 74–75.

pp. 16.

X. LaMotte Sage, *Hypnotism as It Is: A Book for Everybody* (New York, 1897), p. 7; William A. Barnes, *Psychology, Hypnotism, Personal Magnetism and Clairvoyance* (Boston, 1900), p. 41, 53; Stanley LeFevre Krebs, *The Law of Suggestion: A Compendium for the People* (Chicago, 1901), pp. 48ff., 157; R. Osgood Mason, *Hypnotism and Suggestion in Therapeutics, Education and Reform* (New York, 1901), pp. 317–18. Walter Dill Scott's early books are *The Theory of Advertising* (Boston, 1904), *The Psychology of Public Speaking* (Philadelphia, 1907), see p. 175, and *The Psychology of Advertising* (Boston, 1908). See also Hugo Munsterberg, *Business Psychology* (Chicago, 1915), pp. 157–65; Hugo Munsterberg, *The Photoplay: A Psychological Study* (New York, 1916), pp. 22, 28, 110.

pp. 16–17.

Gustavus Ohlinger, "Prussianizing American Schools," *Bookman* 48 (December 1918): pp. 415–22; George Sylvester Viereck, *Spreading Germs of Hate* (New York, 1930); V. F. Calverton, "Our Hypnotized World," *Scribner's Magazine* 101 (April 1937); Emile Coue, *My Method, Including American Impressions* (New York, 1923); Charles Baudouin, *Emile Coue and His Life Work* (New York, 1923), p. 11; Frederick Pierce, *Our Unconscious Mind and How to Use It* (New York, 1922); Frederick Pierce, *Mobilizing the Mid-Brain* (New York, 1924); James Alexander,

Thought-Control in Everyday Life (New York, 1928), pp. 235ff.; Donald Meyer, *The Positive Thinkers* (Garden City, NY, 1965), pp. 21–38, 167–68, 88–90 passim; Joseph Jastrow, *The Psychology of Conviction: A Study of Beliefs and Attitudes* (Boston, 1918), p. 84; Robert W. Marks, *The Story of Hypnotism* (New York, 1947), pp. 233, viii, 194.

CHAPTER 3. THE EROSION OF COMMUNITY IN A DISTENDED SOCIETY

Two books that significantly informed this chapter are Robert Wiebe, *The Search for Order: 1887–1920*, esp. chap. 2, and Graham Wallas, *The Great Society; A Psychological Analysis* (London, 1914), pp. 1, 226ff., 240, 262, 264.

pp. 19–20

Wilson is quoted by Graham Wallas in *Human Nature in Politics*, p. 264. Charles H. Cooley, *Human Nature and Social Order* (New York, 1902), pp. 97–98; Charles H. Cooley, *Social Organization* (New York, 1909), pp. 83ff., 113–17, 172–75; James Bryce, *Modern Democracies*, vol. 2 (New York, 1921), pp. 459–84; Frederic Toennies, *Kritik der Offentlichen Meinung* (Berlin, 1922); Adolph Hitler, *Mein Kampf* (Munich, 1925), trans. Ralph Mannheim (Cambridge, MA, 1943), pp. 88–89; Randolph Bourne, *War and the Intellectuals*, 107ff.; Harold D. Lasswell, *Propaganda Technique in the World War* (New York, 1927), pp. 221–22; John Dewey, "Education as Politics," *New Republic* 32 (October 4, 1922): pp. 139–41; John Dewey, *The Public and Its Problems* (New York, 1927), pp. 109–27.

pp. 21–22.

Harold Innis, *Changing Concepts of Time* (Toronto, 1952), p. 102; Frederick Dwight, "The Significance of Advertising," *Yale Review* (August 1909): pp. 197–205; Edward A. Ross, *Social Control* (New York, 1901), pp. 432–35, 77–80ff., 38; Edward A. Ross, *Sin and Society: An Analysis of Latter Day Iniquity* (Boston, 1908), pp. 63ff.; Edward A. Ross, *Social Psychology* (New York, 1908), pp. 25, 63ff. Walter Dill Scott's early writings are described in the note above relating to chap. 2 of this volume. His later book is *Influencing Men in Business* (New York, 1911). See also Leonard W. Ferguson, *Walter Dill Scott, First Industrial Psychologist* (Hartford, 1952); John Gunther, *Taken at the Flood: The Story of Albert D. Lasker* (New York, 1960), pp. 58ff.; Claude Hopkins, *My Life in Advertising* (New York, 1927).

pp. 22–23.

Adolph Hitler, *Mein Kampf*, pp. 434–75. On revivalism, see William O. McLoughlin, *Modern Revivalism: Charles Grandison Finney to Billy Graham* (New York, 1959); William O. McLoughlin, *Billy Sunday Was His Real Name* (Chicago, 1955). W. I. Thomas, "The Psychology of Yellow Journalism," *American Magazine* 65 (March, 1908): pp. 496ff.; W. I. Thomas, "Billy Sundayism," *Electric Railway Journal* 50 (August 11, 1917): pp. 23–40. Sunday's prayer is cited in Peter Odegard, *The American Public Mind* (New York, 1930), pp. 196–97. See also Helen Woodward, *Through Many Windows* (New York, 1926), p. 289; Helen Woodward, *It's an Art* (New York, 1938); Bruce Barton, *The Man Nobody Knows* (Indianapolis, 1925); Herbert Croly, *The Promise of American Life* (New York, 1909), pp. 451–53. (The *Time* magazine article on Billy Graham is from June 10, 1966, p. 87.)

pp. 23.

Thorstein Veblen, *Absentee Ownership and Business Enterprise in Recent Times* (New York, 1923), pp. 319–25; Silas Bent, *Ballyhoo: The Voice of the Press* (New York, 1927), pp. 319ff.; Charles Stelzle, *Christianity's Storm Center: A Study of the Modern City* (New York, 1907), pp. 36–38; Charles Stelzle, *Principles of Successful Church Publicity* (New York, 1908); Charles Stelzle, "Promotion and Publicity," *Outlook* 143 (June 16, 1926): pp. 252–56; John J. Burke, "Publicity and Social Reform," *Catholic World* 91 (May 1910): pp. 198–211.

pp. 24.

Edward L. Bernays, *Propaganda* (New York, 1928), p. 135; John A. Kingsbury, "Scoops and Nature of Publicity as a Factor in Popular Educational Movements in Public Health," *American Journal of Public Hygiene* 20 (August 1910): pp. 506–15; Edward A. Moore, "Public Health and Public Politics," *Annals* 64 (March 1916): pp. 134–35; F. M. Hall, "Publicity and the Public Health," *American Journal of Public Health* 4 (February 1914): pp. 105–7; Arthur T. Vance, "The Value of Publicity in Reform," *Annals* 29 (January 1907); Vera Whitehouse, *A Year as* a *Government Agent* (New York, 1920); Scott Cutlip, *Fund Raising in the United States* (New Brunswick, NJ, 1965); A. Lawrence Lowell, *Public Opinion in War and Peace* (Cambridge, MA, 1923), p. 40.

pp. 45.

Peter Lyon, *Success Story: The Life and Times of S. S. McClure* (New York, 1963), pp. 281ff.; Samuel Hopkins Adams, "The Great American Fraud," *Collier's* 36 (October 7, 1905–February 17, 1906); Ray Stannard Baker, "How Railroads Make Public Opinion," *McClure's* 16 (March 1906): pp. 535–49; Ray Stannard Baker, "Manufacturing Public Opinion," editorial, *McClure's* 26 (February 1906): pp. 450–52; J. J. Dickinson, "Theodore Roosevelt: Press Agent," *Harper's Weekly* 5 (September 28, 1907): pp. 1410ff.; Letter of Theodore Roosevelt to E. A. Van Valkenberg, quoted in Rush Welter, *Popular Education* (New York, 1965), p. 351ff.; Richard Hofstader, *The American Political Tradition and the Men Who Made It* (New York, 1940), p. 211.

pp. 25–26.

Stanley Kelley, *Professional Public Relations and Political Power* (Baltimore, 1956), p. 28; George Kibbe Turner, "Manufacturing Public Opinion, *McClure's* 39 (July 1912): pp. 316–27; George Kibbe Turner, "Popular Discussion," *New Republic* 4 (August 14, 1915): pp. 35–36; Harold D. Lasswell, *Politics: Who Gets What, When and How* (New York, 1936), part 2; Walter Weyl, *The New Democracy* (New York, 1912), pp. 351, 136.

CHAPTER 4. IVY LEE: THE PATRICIAN PROPAGANDIST

pp. 27–28.

Biographical material about Ivy Lee is based on Ray Eldon Hiebert, *Courtier to the Crowd: The Story of Ivy Lee and the Development of Public Relations* (Ames, IA, 1966), esp. pp. 15–46, 231–38, 138–97, 218–20. Hereafter cited as Hiebert, Biography. Hiebert's doctoral dissertation by the same title (hereafter cited as Hiebert, Dissertation) was completed at the University of Michigan in 1962 and contains some additional information. See esp. pp. 201–20. Eric Goldman, *Two-Way Street: The Emergence of the Public Relations Counsel* (Boston, 1948), pp. 5–7; Ivy Lee, *Publicity for Public Service Corporations* (New York, 1916), pp. 1–11; Ivy Lee, "The Technique of Publicity," *Electric Railway Journal* 49 (January 6, 1917): pp. 16–18; Ivy Lee, *The American Railroad Problem* (London, 1910), p. 23; Ivy Lee, *The Problem of International Propaganda* (New York, 1934), pp. 3ff.

pp. 28–29.

Ray Hiebert, Biography, pp. 163, 234–318; see also US Congress, House of Representatives, *Special Committee on Un-American Activities, Investigation of Nazi Propaganda,,* 73rd Congress, 2nd Session, 1934, esp. vol. 7, pp. 176–205; John Price Jones with David M. Church, *At the Bar of Public Opinion* (New York, 1939), pp. 1–8; T. N. Vail, "Views on Public Questions," *A Collection of Papers and Addresses, 1907–1917* (privately printed, 1917), p. 243; editorial, *Electric Railway Journal* 47 (January 1, 1916); A. J. Eddy, quoted in Cochran, *The American Business System*, p. 61; Henry Clews, "Publicity and Reform in Business," *Annals* 28 (July 1906): pp. 143–54; D. F. Wilcox, "The American Newspaper," *Annals* 16 (July 1900): pp. 56–92; Jeremiah Jenks, "The Guidance of Public Opinion," *American Journal of Sociology* 1 (September 1895): pp. 158–69.

pp. 29–30.

See Paul Arthur Palmer, "The Concept of Public Opinion in Political Thought," in *Essays in History and Political Theory in Honor of Charles Howard McIlwain* (Cambridge, MA, 1936); Albert Vann Dicey, quoted in Robert W. Park and Ernest W. Burgess, *Introduction to the Science of Sociology* (Chicago, 1921), pp. 449, 791; Charles H. Cooley, *Social Organization*, p. 131; M. A. DeWolfe Howe, *Public Opinion, Directed and Impelled …* (Hartford, CT, 1852), p. 16; James Garfield, quoted in Graham Wallas, *Human Nature in Politics*, pp. 111–12; Robert M. LaFollette in the *Congressional Record*, vol. 61, part 6 (October 18, 1921), p. 6337; Robert M. LaFollette, *LaFollette's Magazine* (October 1916): p. 1; James Bryce, *Modern Democracies*, vol. 1 (New York, 1931), pp. 156ff.; T. V. Smith, "The Voice of the People," *Annals* 169 (September 1933): p. 109; Walter Lippmann, *Public Opinion* (New York, 1922), pp. 255ff.

pp. 31–33.

Ivy Lee, *Publicity for Public Service Corporations*, pp. 46, 61, 15; Ivy Lee, *Publicity: Some of the Things It Is and Is Not* (New York, 1925), pp. 23, 36; Ray Hiebert, Dissertation, p. 296; Ray Hiebert, Biography, p. 307; Ivy Lee, "The Human Nature of Publicity," *Electric Railway Journal* 50 (August 14, 1917): pp. 181–82; Ivy Lee, *Publicity for Public Service Corporations*, p. 21; Ray Hiebert, Biography, pp. 17, 226–27, 22–29, 272–83, 160; Ivy Lee, *Present Day Russia*

(New York, 1928); Ivy Lee, "Indirect Service of Railroads," *Moody's Magazine* (November 1907): pp. 580-84; Ray Hiebert, Dissertation, pp. 24, 100, 148-51; Eric Goldman, *Two-Way Street*, pp. 7-9.

pp. 34-35.

M. K. Wisehart, "How Big Men Think and Act," *American Magazine* 108 (July 1929): pp. 126-27. See also Rockefeller-Lee correspondence in US Congress, Senate, Commission on Industrial Relations, *Final Report and Testimony*, 64th Congress, 2nd Session, 1916, vol. 7, pp. 8871-81; Raymond D. Fosdick, *John D. Rockefeller, Jr.: A Portrait* (New York, 1956); Ray Hiebert, Biography, pp. 97-108, 125-34, 146, 69; Ivy Lee, *Publicity for Public Service Corporations*, p. 7; Ivy Lee, "The Technique of Publicity," pp. 16-18; Ivy Lee, "Advertising in Publicity Work," *Electric Railway Journal* 50 (October 7, 1917): p. 618; John K. Mumford, *A Physician to Corporate Bodies* (New York, 1925), pp. 15-17; John K. Mumford, "Bridge in Business," *Editor & Publisher* 7 (January 18, 1908): p. 2; Ray Hiebert, Dissertation, p. 224.

pp. 35-39.

Wayne W. Parrish, "Ivy Lee, 'Family Physician to Big Business,'" *Literary Digest* 117 (June 9, 1934): pp. 30ff.; Ray Hiebert, Biography, p. 315; Ray Hiebert, Dissertation, p. 171; Ivy Lee, *Publicity*, pp. 15-30; Ray Hiebert, Dissertation, pp. 219, 15, 159, 175; Ivy Lee, *Publicity and the Public Service Corporations*, p. 47; Ivy Lee, "Principles Underlying Publicity," pp. 663-65; Ivy Lee, *Human Nature and the Railroads* (Philadelphia, 1915), pp. 14-16; Ivy Lee, "The Human Nature of Publicity," pp. 181-82; Ivy Lee, *International Propaganda*, pp. 8, 23, 12; Ivy Lee, and *Publicity*, p. 36; Ivy Lee, "Modern Lawyer," *World's Work* 8 (June 1904): p. 4879; Ray Hiebert, Biography, pp. 298-300; Letter of Felix Frankfurter to Franklin D. Roosevelt, *Roosevelt and Frankfurter: Their Correspondence, 1928-1945*, annotator Max Freedman (Boston, 1967), p. 214; Ivy Lee, *Human Nature and the Railroads*, p. 56; US *Congressional Record*, 63rd Congress, 2nd Session, 1914, vol. 51, part 8, pp. 7735ff., 8859ff.; "The Enemies of Publicity," *Electric Railway Journal* 49 (March 31, 1917): p. 600.

CHAPTER 5. THE PROPAGANDIST AS PROGRESSIVE WARRIOR

pp. 41-43.

Creel's own writings are the basis for this chapter, including *How We Advertised America* (New York, 1920), and *Rebel at Large: Recollections of Fifty Crowded Years* (New York, 1957), with his early years summed up in pp. 1-80 of the latter volume. A particularly comprehensive and compelling description of American opinion—and efforts to influence it before and during the Great War—is found in David M. Kennedy, *Over Here: The First World War and American Society* (Oxford, 1980, 25th anniversary edition published in New York, 2004). Also providing detailed coverage of Creel and the Committee on Public Information is James R. Mock and Cedric Larson, *Words That Won the War: The Story of the Committee on Public Information, 1917-1919* (Princeton, 1939); and more recently, Alan Axelrod, *Selling the Great War: The Making of American Propaganda* (New York, 2009); George Creel, *Quatrains of Christ* (San Francisco, 1908); Mock and Larson, *Words That Won the War*, p. 51; George Creel, *Rebel at Large*, pp. 80-145; George Creel, "Poisoners of Public Opinion," *Harper's Weekly* 59 (November 7 and 14, 1914): pp. 46-438, 465-66; Paul Kellogg, "Muckraked," *New Republic* 2 (February 29, 1915): pp. 60-61; "George Creel Replies," *New Republic* 2 (March 27, 1915): pp. 209-10; George Creel, *Rebel at Large*, pp. 123ff.; George Creel, *Wilson and the Issues* (New York, 1916); pp. 4-9, 57ff., 148ff.; Mock and Larson, *Words That Won the War*, pp. 11, 49-50; Mark Sullivan, *Our Times: The United States, 1900-1925*, vol. 5, *Over Here: 1914-1918* (New York, 1926-1935), p. 370.

pp. 44-47.

Will Irwin, *Propaganda and the News, or What Makes You Think So?* (New York, 1936), p. 124; Mark Sullivan, *Over Here*, p. 66; George Sylvester Viereck, *Spreading Germs of Hate* (New York, 1930), p. 168. Among the many early analyses of German and British propaganda before 1917 are H. C. Peterson, *Propaganda for War: The Campaign against American Neutrality, 1914-1917* (Norman, OK, 1939); James Morgan Read, *Atrocity Propaganda, 1914-1919* (New Haven, CT, 1941); and James D. Squires, *British Propaganda at Home and in the United States from 1914-1917* (Cambridge, MA, 1935). See also, for example, Harold D. Lasswell, *Propaganda Technique in the World War* (New York, 1927); Barry Allen Marks, "The Idea of Propaganda in America" (unpublished PhD diss., University of Minnesota, 1957). The comment by Upton Sinclair is found in his *Money Writes! A Study of American Literature* (Long Beach, CA, 1927), p. 25. See also Gilbert Parker, "The United States and the War," *Harper's Magazine* 136 (March 1918): pp. 521-31.

pp. 45–47.

Mark Sullivan, *Over Here*, p. 434; Edward L. Bernays, *Biography of an Idea: Memoirs of Public Relations Counsel, Edward L. Bernays* (New York, 1965), p. 157; George Creel, *How We Advertised America*, pp. 79, 84, 101, 250; G. S. Ford, "America's Fight for Public Opinion," *Minnesota History Bulletin* 3 (1919): pp. 3–26; G. S. Ford, "The Committee on Public Information," *Historical Outlook* 11 (March 1920): pp. 97–100; Oswald Garrison Villard, *Fighting Years: Memoirs of a Liberal Editor* (New York, 1939), p. 523; George Sylvester Viereck, *Spreading Germs of Hate*, p. 296; Mock and Larson, *Words That Won the War*, pp. 6–8; "Government and Propaganda," *Nation* 108 (March 1, 1919): p. 313.

pp. 47–52.

George Creel, *How We Advertised America*, pp. 62, 3–15, 112; George Creel, *Complete Report of the Committee on Public Information* (Washington, DC, 1920), pp. 6ff.; Mock and Larson, *Words That Won the War*, pp. 6–8, 113; Mark Sullivan, *Our Times*, pp. 434ff.; "Government and Propaganda," *Nation* 108 (March 1, 1919): p. 313; Mark Sullivan, "Creel-Censor," *Collier's* 60 (November 10, 1917): pp. 13, 36–37; Mark Sullivan, *Over Here*, pp. 365–66, 426; Mark and Larson, *Words That Won the War*, p. 55; George Creel, "Propaganda and Morale," *American Journal of Sociology* 47 (November 1941): pp. 340–51; George Creel, "Creel: An Announcement," *Everybody's* 40 (January 1919): p. 25; George Creel, *How We Advertised America*, chap. 5; George Creel, "The Lash of Public Opinion," *Collier's* 74 (November 22, 1924): pp. 8–9ff.; Mark Sullivan, "Creel-Censor," pp. 35–37; George Creel, *The War, the World and Wilson* (New York, 1920), pp. 119ff., 3ff.; E. T. Saintsbury, "Memoirs of a Four Minute Man," *American Mercury* 10 (March 1927): pp. 284–91; George Creel, *Wilson and the Issues*, pp. 148, 57; George Creel, *The War, the World and Wilson*, pp. 55, 119, 11–19, 133ff., chap. 15; George Creel, *How We Advertised America*, pp. 9, xi–xviii, 3–5, 140 (where the Irwin poem is reprinted).

pp. 53–54.

George Creel, *Ireland's Fight for Freedom* (New York, 1919), p. xiii; George Creel, "The Lash of Public Opinion," pp. 46ff.; George Creel, *Uncle Henry*, published anonymously (New York, 1922), p. 240; George Creel, *The War, the World and Wilson*, pp. 163–64; George Sylvester Viereck, *Spreading Germs of Hate*, p. 95; Edward L. Bernays, *Biography*, p. 155; George Creel, *How We Advertised America*, chaps. 3–4, esp. p. 50. Among Will Irwin's recollections, see, for example, Will Irwin, "An Age of Lies," *Sunset* 48 (1919): p. 54; Will Irwin, "If You See It in the Paper, It's—?," *Colliers's* 72 (August 18, 1923): pp. 11ff.; and his later books, Will Irwin, *Propaganda and the News*, esp. p. 185; Will Irwin, *The Making of a Reporter* (New York, 1942), p. 353. See also George Creel, "Propaganda and Morale," p. 349; George Creel, *Report of the Chairman*, pp. 11–12; George Creel, "Public Opinion in War Time," p. 187; George Creel, "The Plight of the Last Censor," *Collier's* 107 (May 24, 1941): pp. 13, 34–36; George Creel, *Rebel at Large*, pp. 160–70; Harold Lasswell, *Propaganda Technique in the World War*, p. 28; George Creel, *How We Advertised America*, pp. 21–23; George Creel, "The American Newspaper: What It Is and What it Isn't," *Everybody's* 40 (April 1919): pp. 40–44.

pp. 54.

George Creel, "Public Opinion in War Time," p. 185; Arthur S. Link, *American Epoch: A History of the United States since the 1890's* (New York, 1955), p. 215; Frank Luther Mott, *American Journalism* (New York, 1950), p. 627; George Creel, "Public Opinion in War Time," pp. 187–92; George Creel, *How We Advertised America*, appendix, pp. 443–52; George Creel, "The Fight for Public Opinion," *Scientific Monthly* 118 (April 6, 2018): p. 298; Mock and Larson, *Words That Won the War*, pp. 13–18; "The Problem of Morale," *New Republic* 14 (April 27, 1918): pp. 374–75; *New Republic* 14 (February 9, 1918): p. 37.

pp. 54–58.

George Creel, *How We Advertised America*, pp. 16–19; Newton D. Baker, forward to *How We Advertised America*, by George Creel, p. xiv. See also Paul Campbell Young, "Suggestion as Indirection," *Journal of Abnormal and Social Psychology* 26 (April–June, 1931): pp. 69–90, which reviews the relevant literature of the period. C. H. Hamlin, *The War Myth in United States History* (New York, 1927), p. 91. An excellent summary of the backlash against Creel is found in Barry Allen Marks, "The Idea of Propaganda," pp. 21ff., 53ff. See also Heber Blankenhorn, *Adventures in Propaganda: Letter from an Intelligence Officer in France* (Boston, 1919), p. 48; George Seldes, *Freedom of the Press* (Indianapolis, 1937), p. 35. George Creel, *How We Advertised America*, pp. 63–69; Arthur S. Link, *Wilson: The New Freedom* (Princeton, 1956), p. 79; H. L. Mencken, "The Archangel Woodrow," *Smart Set* (January 1921), reprinted in Alistair Cook, ed., *The Vintage Mencken* (New York, 1955), pp. 116–20; Arthur S. Link, *Wilson: The Road to the White House* (Princeton, 1947), p. 5; Henry A. Turner, "Woodrow Wilson and Public Opinion," *Public Opinion Quarterly* 21 (Winter 1957–1958): pp. 505–20; Sigmund

Freud and William C. Bullitt, *Thomas Woodrow Wilson* (Boston, 1966), pp. 3, 18–22, 52, 193–94, 284–85; H. C. Lodge, quoted in US General Staff, Military Intelligence Branch, *Propaganda in Its Military and Legal Aspects* (Washington, DC, 1919), pp. 150ff.

pp. 59–60.

Quotations from Wilson are taken from his own books, *Congressional Government, A Study in American Politics* (New York, 1885, republished—with an introduction by Walter Lippmann—in New York and Cleveland, 2006); *Constitutional Government in the United States* (New York, 1908); and from secondary treatments, primarily Arthur S. Link, *The Road to the White House* and *The New Freedom*. Roosevelt's comment is reported in Mark Sullivan, *Over Here*, p. 482. See also George Creel, *The War, the World and Wilson*, pp. 18–19; Henry A. Turner, "Woodrow Wilson and Public Opinion," pp. 525–16; John Morton Blum, *Joe Tumulty and the Wilson Era* (Boston, 1951), pp. 55ff., 170–71; Elmer E. Cornwell Jr., "Wilson, Creel and the Presidency," *Public Opinion Quarterly* 23 (Summer 1959): pp. 189–202; Harold D. Lasswell, *Propaganda Technique in the World War*, pp. 216–19. Woodrow Wilson, *Constitutional Government*, pp. 117–20; Arthur S. Link, *The Road to the White House*, p. 83; George Creel, *How We Advertised America*, pp. 108, 65–66; Martin Conway, *The Crowd in Peace and War*, pp. 97ff.; Perry Miller, "Revivalism," in *Jonathan Edwards* (New York, 1949), pp. 133–63.

pp. 60–62.

John Dewey, "Theodore Roosevelt," *Dial* (February 8, 1918), reprinted in Joseph Ratner, ed. *Characters and Events*, vol. 1 (New York, 1929), p. 87; also "Democratic Diplomacy," (January 19, 2018): p. 329; and also issues of August 24, 1918, and May 4, 1918; Christopher Lasch, *The New Radicalism in America, 1889–1963: The Intellectual as a Social Type* (New York, 1965), chaps. 5–6, esp. pp. 161–62; Frederick William Wile, "Government by Propaganda," *Outlook and Independent* 150 (December 26, 1928): pp. 1387–98, 1417, 1422. See also Gene Smith, *When the Cheering Stopped* (New York, 1964), part 1, a lively narrative. More reliable detail is found in Thomas A. Bailey, *Woodrow Wilson and the Great Betrayal* (New York, 1945), chaps. 6–8. George Creel, *How We Advertised America*, p. 105; Elmer E. Cornwell Jr., "Wilson, Creel and the Presidency," p. 197. See also David Kennedy, afterword to the 2004 edition of *Over Here: The First World War and American Society*, in which he discusses Wilson's aspirations to be the voice of America's inherited exceptionalist identity, along with his longer-range impact in translating that dimension of American consciousness onto the world stage. A recent illuminating study of American attitudes regarding the war is Andrew J. Huebner, *Love and Death in the Great War* (Oxford, 2018).

CHAPTER 6. THE PROPAGANDIST AS EDUCATOR— AND VICE VERSA

pp. 63–64.

Arnold Bennett Hall, excerpted in W. B. Graves, ed., *Readings in Public Opinion* (New York, 1927), pp. 923–27; David Noble, *The Paradox of Progressive Thought* (Minneapolis, MN, 1958); Charles McCarthy, *The Wisconsin Idea* (New York, 1912). Josiah Strong, *Twentieth Century City* (New York, 1898); Robert C. Brooks, *Political Parties and Electoral Problems* (New York, 1913). The states passing information laws were Oregon and Montana (1907); Oklahoma (1908); California (1909); Arizona (1912); Colorado, Nebraska, Ohio, and Washington (1913); Utah (1917); and North Dakota and Massachusetts (1918). See also *Electric Railway Journal* 51 (January 12, 1918): pp. 69ff.; "Publicity without Candor," *New Republic* 29 (December 7, 1921): p. 29; Bruce Bliven, "The Ether Will Now Oblige," *New Republic* 29 (February 15, 1922): pp. 328–30; Walter Lippmann, "Blazing Publicity," in *Vanity Fair: Selections from American's Most Memorable Magazine*, ed. Cleveland Amory and Frederick Bradlee (New York, 1960), pp. 121–22; Edward S. Martin, "Advertisement," *Atlantic Monthly* 53 (January 1909): pp. 36–39; Gerald Stanley Lee, *Inspired Millionaires* (Northampton, MA, 1908), pp. 288, 272.

pp. 65–66.

George Sylvester Viereck, *Spreading Germs of Hate*, pp. 296ff.; Frederick Lumley, "Slogans as a Means of Social Control," *Publications of the American Sociological Society* 16 (1921); Frederick Lumley, *The Propaganda Menace* (New York, 1933), p. 222; Carl Sandburg, *The People, Yes* (New York, 1936), pp. 280–81; Neil MacNeil, *Without Fear or Favor* (New York, 1940), p. 300; Martin Conway, *The Crowd in Peace and War*, p. 37; A. P. Lipsky, *Man the Puppet* (New York, 1925), pp. 33–34; *New York Tribune* (July 12, 1918), quoted in Harold D. Lasswell, *Propaganda Technique*, p. 209; Frank R. Cobb, "Public Opinion," address to the Women's City Club of New York, December 11, 1919, reprinted by US Congress, 66th Congress, 2nd Session: Senate Document 175 (Washington, DC, 1920), pp. 3–5; Edward L. Munson, *The Management of Men: A Handbook on the Systematic Development of Morale and the Control of Human Behavior* (New York, 1921), p. v; Stuart Hanson of Radio Free Europe at Notre Dame University, November 20, 1961, quoted in George N. Gordon, Irving Falk, and William Hodapp, *The Idea Invaders* (New York, 1963), p. 165.

pp. 66–69.

Harold D. Lasswell, quoted in Elmer Ellis, ed., *Education against Propaganda* (New York, 1937), p. 25; Harold D. Lasswell, *Propaganda Technique*, pp. 2–3; O. W. Reigel, "Propaganda and the Press," *Annals* 179 (May, 1925): p. 201; James B. Conant, "Defenses against Propaganda," *Vital Speeches* 4 (June 15, 1938): p. 542; Will Irwin, *Propaganda and the News*, p. 239. Various definitions of *propaganda* are discussed in Frederick Lumley, *Propaganda Menace*, pp. 20ff.; Terence H. Qualter, *Propaganda and Psychological Warfare* (New York, 1962), pp. 6–31. Agnes Repplier, "A Good Word Gone Wrong," *Independent* 57 (October 1, 1921): p. 5; Leonard W. Doob, *Propaganda: Its Psychology and Technique* (New York, 1935), pp. 83ff., 200, 8–9; Frederick Lumley, *Propaganda Menace*, pp. 121, 390; James Mark Baldwin, *Social and Ethical Interpretations in Mental Development* (New York, 1897), pp. 542ff.; George E. Vincent, *The Social Mind and Education* (New York, 1897); Graham Wallas, *The Great Society*, pp. 16–134; Charles H. Cooley, *Human Nature and the Social Order* (New York, 1902); Charles H. Cooley, *Social Organization: A Study of the Larger Mind* (New York, 1909), chap. 3. See also Charles E. Ellwood, *The Psychology of Human Society: An Introduction to Sociological Theory* (New York, 1925); and Charles E. Ellwood, "Charles Horton Cooley, Sociologist, 1864–1929," *Sociology and Social Research* 14 (September–October 1929): pp. 3–9, which describes Dewey's impact on Cooley.

pp. 69–70.

John Dewey, "The People and the Schools," *Educational Review* (May 1901); John Dewey, *The School and Society* (Chicago, 1899), p. 59; John Dewey, *Democracy and Education: An Introduction to the Philosophy of Education* (New York, 1916), pp. 12ff., 30–39; John Dewey, "Education and Social Direction," *Dial* (April 18, 1918). Some of Dewey's insights are reprinted in Joseph Ratner, ed., *Education Today* (New York, 1940). Other useful sources are John Dewey, "Public Opinion in War Time," *New Republic* 12 (September 22, 1917): pp. 204–7; John Dewey, *School and Society* (Chicago, 1902); John Dewey, *The Child and the Curriculum* (Chicago, 1902); and John Dewey, *Reconstruction in Philosophy* (New York, 1920). The three *New Republic* articles are from vol. 32, the issues of September 13, September 20, and October 4, 1920. See also John Dewey, *My Pedagogic Creed* (Washington, DC, 1931), p. 17.

pp. 71–74.

Sidney Hook, *John Dewey: An Intellectual Portrait* (New York, 1939), p. 159; John Dewey, "A New World in the Making," *New Republic* 57 (November 28, 1928): p. 41; Christopher Lasch, *The New Radicalism in America*, pp. 155ff., 202ff.; John Dewey, *The Public and Its Problems*, pp. 184ff.; George S. Counts, *Dare the Schools Build a New Social Order?* (New York, 1931), pp. 6, 28; Karl Wallace, ed., *History of Speech Education in America* (New York, 1954); Mary P. Follett, *The New State, Group Organization: The Solution of Popular Government* (New York, 1918); Seba Eldridge, *The Art of Citizenship* (New York, 1929); A. D. Sheffield, *Joining in Public Discussion* (New York, 1922), pp. vi ff.; Harrison Sacket Elliott, *The Process of Group Thinking* (New York, 1928), p. 15; Maria Montessori, *The Montessori Method*, trans. Anne E. George (New York, 1912), esp. pp. 115–17, 210–11; Charles H. Cooley, *Social Process*, p. 105ff.; Carl Byoir, "The Presentation of Montessori Material," *Journal of Proceedings and Addresses of the National Education Association*, 50th annual meeting, July 1912 (Chicago, 1912), pp. 613–21; George Creel, *How We Advertised America*, p. 248; Ray Hiebert, *Biography*, p. 293; Spencer Klaw, "Carl Byoir: Opinion Engineering in the Big Time," *Reporter* 6 (June 10, 1952); John Dewey and Evelyn Dewey, *Schools of Tomorrow* (New York, 1915), pp. 290ff.

CHAPTER 7. EDWARD BERNAYS AND THE ENGINEERING OF CONSENT

pp. 75.

Much of the biographical material in this chapter is based on Edward Bernays's own memoir, *Biography of an Idea: Memoirs of Public Relations Counsel, Edward L. Bernays* (New York, 1965). The *New York World* article cited here is referenced on pp. 145–46; see also pp. 287–88. This massive autobiography (816 pages) represents only about half of the manuscript that Bernays prepared after his retirement. Most of his papers are at the Library of Congress, but many referred to in this essay were papers that Bernays made available to this author in Cambridge, Massachusetts, in conjunction with his interview there with Bernays on January 7, 1968. Many letters were originally solicited and gathered to celebrate Bernays's seventieth and seventy-fifth birthdays, in 1961 and 1966. More material from these papers and from that interview is cited in in the author's doctoral dissertation, *The Discovery of Propaganda: Changing Attitudes Toward Public Communication in America, 1900–1930* (PhD diss., Harvard University, 1968). Other particularly useful sources include Bernays's own major books, cited below, and Larry Tye, *The Father of Spin: Edward L. Bernays and the Birth of Public Relations* (New York, 1998).

p. 75–78.

Leonard W. Doob, *Propaganda*, p. 205. See also Eric F. Goldman, *Two-Way Street*, pp. v–vi, 19–20; Bernays, *Biography*, parts I and II, esp. pp. 155–78. The Bliven quotation is from the Bernays papers mentioned above. Irwin Ross, *The Image Merchants: The Fabulous World of Public Relations* (Garden City, NY, 1959), pp. 51, 241; Harwood L. Childs, *A Reference Guide to the Study of Public Opinion* (Princeton, 1934); Eric W. Allen, "The Social Value of a Code of Ethics for Journalists," *Annals* 101 (May, 1922): pp. 170–79; *St. Louis Post Dispatch* (March 8, 1924); Herman Mankiewicz, *New York Times* (April 6, 1924); Ernest Gruening, "The Higher Hokum," *Nation* 68 (April 16, 1924): p. 450; E. E. Calkins, *Business the Civilizer* (Boston, 1928); Stanley Walker, "Playing the Deep Bassoons," *Harper's* 164 (February 1932): pp. 369, 365; and Stanley Walker, *City Editor* (New York, 1934). These and other commentaries cited here were found in the Bernays papers, referenced in Bernays, *Biography*, p. 779, or were part of the author's Bernays interview (1968).

pp. 79–80.

Detailed discussions of specific Bernays public relations projects fill much of his *Biography*, including its appendix. See also p. 290. Other information comes from this author's interview with Bernays of January 7, 1968, and from a talk by Bernays at Kirkland House, Harvard University, March 10, 1966. See also George Seldes, *Lords of the Press* (New York, 1938), p. 304; Edward L. Bernays, *Crystallizing Public Opinion* (New York, 1923); Walter Lippmann, *Public Opinion*, esp. p. 193.

pp. 80–83.

Edward L. Bernays, *Propaganda* (New York, 1928); Edward L. Bernays, *Private Interest and Public Responsibility* (New York, 1939); Edward L. Bernays, Public *Relations* (Norman, OK, 1952), esp. pp. 122–23. See also Edward L. Bernays, "The Press Agent Has His Day," *Printers' Ink* 110 (February 26, 1920): pp. 107–8. Among the writers who wrestled with alternative vocabularies were A. M. Christensen, *Politics and Crowd Morality* (London, 1915); and Joost A. M. Meerloo, *The Rape of the Mind* (Cleveland, OH, 1956). Edward L. Bernays, *Crystalizing Public Opinion*, pp. 147ff., 118–19. The quest for a properly subtle terminology has continued. In his seminal 1999 analysis of the potential role of "public journalism," Jay Rosen faced a similar conceptual issue: how to describe a proactive leadership role for journalists without violating the presumed sovereignty of independent public opinion. The phrase he used, after describing the ways in which public opinion could readily be "broken," was to suggest that the role of responsible public journalists was "to see the public into fuller existence." Jay Rosen, *What Are Journalists For?* (New Haven, 1999).

pp. 84–86.

Edward L. Bernays, *Biography*, pp. 269–70; Edward L. Bernays, *Propaganda*, pp. 9–25; John Carter, "Unseen Empire," *Independent* 121 (July 7 and 14, 1928). Among the many accounts of the FTC investigation are Ernest Gruening, *The Public Pays*; "Propaganda by Public Utility Corporations," *Bulletin of the American Association of University Professors* 16 (May 1930); Federal Trade Commission, *Summary Report on Efforts to Influence Public Opinion* (Washington, DC, 1934); William Bennett Munro, *The Invisible Government* (New York, 1928), pp. 15–16, chap. 4; Edward L. Bernays, interview; Edward L. Bernays, *Propaganda*, pp. 27–32, 92, 114; Edward L. Bernays, *Biography*, pp. 293–94; Edward L. Bernays, "The Minority Rules," *Bookman* 65 (April 1937): pp. 150–55.

pp. 86–87.

Everett Dean Martin, "Our Invisible Masters," *Forum* 81 (March, 1929): pp. 142–45; Henry F. Pringle, "Mass Psychologist," *American Mercury* 19 (February 1930): pp. 155–62; John T. Flynn, "Edward L. Bernays, 'The Science of Ballyhoo," *Atlantic Monthly* 149 (May 1932): pp. 562–71; Leonard Doob, *Propaganda*, p. 200. Edward L. Bernays, interview; Edward L. Bernays, *Biography*. See also Edward L. Bernays, "Needed: A Grand Strategy," *Saturday*

Review of Literature 25 (March 7, 1942): p. 10; and Edward L. Bernays, "Attitude Polls—Servant or Master?," *Public Opinion Quarterly* 9 (Fall 1945). Chase, *Government in Business*, p. 263. Also see Bernays's comments in Anne Sutherland, "Public Relations, Edward L. Bernays and the American Scene. Annotated Bibliography of and Reference Guide to Writings by and About Edward L. Bernays: from 1917–1951," *Bulletin of Bibliography and Dramatic Index* (Boston, 1950).

pp. 87–90.

Edward L. Bernays, ed., *The Engineering of Consent* (Norman, OK, 1955). Also Edward L. Bernays, *Propaganda*, p. 112; Edward L. Bernays, *Crystallizing*, pp. 448ff.; Edward L. Bernays, *Public Relations*, p. 182. Several early uses of the term *engineering* are cited in this author's dissertation referenced earlier, "The Discovery of Propaganda," p. 332. See also Edwin L. Earp, *The Social Engineer* (New York, 1911); Gerald Stanley Lee, *We* (Garden City, NY, 1919); Gerald Stanley Lee, *Crowds: A Moving Picture of Democracy* (Garden City, NY, 1919); Gerald Stanley Lee, *The Ghost in the White House* (New York, 1920). Herbert Newton Casson, *Ads and Sales* (Chicago, 1911), p. 56; Edward L. Bernays, *Biography*; Leonard Doob, *Propaganda*, pp. 199ff.; Elihu Katz and Paul Lazarsfeld, *Personal Influence* (Glencoe, IL, 1955); Scott M. Cutlip, *Fund-Raising in the United States* (New Brunswick, NJ, 1965); Edward L. Bernays, interview; Edward L. Bernays, *Biography*; William A. Biddle, "A Psychological Definition of Propaganda," *Journal of American Abnormal and Social Psychology* 26 (April 1931): pp. 283–95.

pp. 91–94.

Robert Heilbroner, quoted in "The Arts and Uses of Public Relations," *Time* (July 7, 1967); Donald Meyer, *The Positive Thinkers*; Edwin L. Earp, *The Social Engineer*, p. 114; Ivy Lee, *Crowds*, pp. 339–43. Charles Washburn, *Press Agentry*, pp. 31, 43; W. F. Barnard, *The Buying Impulse and How to Lead It* (Cleveland, 1920), p. 16; David M. Potter, *People of Plenty* (Chicago, 1954), p. 59; Bruce Barton, *The Man Nobody Knows*; Arthur Miller, *Death of a Salesman* (New York, 1949), p. 138; Sinclair Lewis, *It Can't Happen Here* (Garden City, NY, 1935), pp. 36, 38; Edward L. Bernays, *Biography*, pp. 646ff.; Dorothy Thompson, *I Saw Hitler* (New York, 1932), pp. 70–71; Ferdinand Lundberg, "Freedom to Distort the Truth," *Forum* 99 (June 1938): pp. 341–45. An extreme version of this critique is found in George Seldes, *The Facts Are* (New York, 1942) when he writes on p. 48 that advertising "in its spirit and practice is germinal Fascism."

pp. 94–96.

Edward L. Bernays, interview. See also Edward L. Bernays, "Public Education for Democracy," *Annals* 198 (July 1938): pp. 124–27; Edward L. Bernays, "How to Restore Public Confidence in Business and Finance," *Economic Forum* (Winter 1936): p. 277; Edward L. Bernays, "Manipulating Public Opinion," p. 960; and other writings cited in Anne Sutherland, *Bibliography*, p. 21. See also Edward L. Bernays, *Public Relations*, p. 9; Edward L. Bernays, *Take Your Place at the Peace Table* (New York, 1945), p. 2. The World's Fair speech is in Bernays's papers, and the *New Yorker* article is quoted in Edward L. Bernays, *Biography*, p. 604–5. See also Irwin Ross, *The Image Merchants*, pp. 255ff.; Neil MacNeil, *Without Fear or Favor* (New York, 1940), pp. 309–14ff.; Herbert Croly, *The Promise of American Life* (New York, 1909), p. 454; Edward L. Bernays, interview, Edward L. Bernays, *Biography*, epigraph; John Milton, *Samson Agonistes: The Poetical Works of John Milton*, ed. H. C. Breeching (Oxford, 1904, new edition, 1938), pp. 529–30. The Biblical story on which Milton's poem is based in found in the book of Judges, chap. 16.

CHAPTER 8. WALTER LIPPMANN'S UNBLINKING REALISM

pp. 97–98.

The major biography of Lippmann is by Ronald Steel, *Walter Lippmann and the American Century, New Edition* (London, 2017). Helpful earlier essays on Lippmann's life appear in Marquis Childs and James Reston, eds., *Walter Lippmann and His Times* (New York, 1959), including Arthur M. Schlesinger Jr., "Walter Lippmann: The Intellectual v. Politics." Lippmann's early books cited here are *A Preface to Politics* (New York, 1913) and *Drift and Mastery* (New York, 1914). See also William E. Leuchtenburg, introduction to *Walter Lippmann, Drift and Mastery* (Englewood Cliffs, NJ, 1961); Charles Forcey, *The Crossroads of Liberalism: Croly, Weyl, Lippmann and the Progressive Era, 1900–1925* (New York, 1961), esp. pp. 88–118. See also Graham Wallas, *Human Nature in Politics*; Graham Wallas, *The Great Society*.

pp. 98-102.

Walter Lippmann, *Preface to Politics*, pp. 67–69, 77–82; Charles Forcey, *Crossroads of Liberalism*, p. 116; Walter Lippmann, *Drift and Mastery*, pp. 272–76, 289ff., 316–33, 121–32, 143–47, 149–57, xviii–xxi. "The world has suffered more from leaders and authorities than from the masses," John Dewey echoed in *The Public and Its Problems*, p. 208. Walter Lippmann, *Preface to Politics*, pp. 246–51, 289–98, 317–18, 91–101, 106–9, 168–78, 294–313; Graham Wallas, *Human Nature in Politics*, pp. 88–99; Charles Forcey, *Crossroads of Liberalism*, pp. 116ff.

pp. 102-106.

Walter Lippmann, *Drift and Mastery*, pp. 40–49, 66–70, 209–12, 61–64, 283–88. At the midpoint of Wilson's presidency, Lippmann incisively shared his views in "Washington Notes," *New Republic* 5 (January 15, 1916): pp. 278–79. Lippmann's later books, mentioned here and also cited later, include *Public Opinion* (New York, 1922), *The Phantom Public* (New York, 1925), *A Preface to Morals* (New York, 1929), *The Method of Freedom* (New York, 1934), *The Good Society* (Boston, 1937), and *Essays in the Public Philosophy* (Boston, 1955). See also Arthur M. Schlesinger Jr., "Walter Lippmann," p. 200; Walter Lippmann, "Unrest," *New Republic* 20 (November 12, 1919): pp. 315–22, Walter Lippmann with Charles Merz, "A Test of the News," *New Republic* 23 (August 4, 1920), Special Supplement.

pp. 106-107.

Walter Lippmann, "The Crude Barbarian and the Noble Savage," and "The Group Mind," *New Republic* 25 (December 15, 1920): pp. 70–71, 82–86; Walter Lippmann, "The Behavior of Crowds," *New Republic* 26 (March 2, 1921): pp. 22–23; Sidney Brooks, "The Press in War Time," *North American Review* 200 (December 1914). Arthur M. Schlesinger Jr., "Walter Lippmann," p. 202; John Dewey, "Public Opinion," *New Republic* 30 (May 3, 1922): pp. 286–88; Walter Lippmann, *Public Opinion*, esp. chaps. 1, 6, 17, and pp. 90, 104–14, 197–203, 215, 219, 234–37. On this theme see also Raymond Dodge, "Psychology of Propaganda," *Religious Education* 15 (October 1920): pp. 241–52, an able statement by a professor of psychology at Wesleyan who touches on, almost as though it were common knowledge, much of what Lippmann was about to articulate.

pp. 107.

One of the most striking later descriptions of the stereotype concept was that of Orson Welles after his famous Martian invasion broadcast of 1938: "The forceps of our minds are clumsy forceps," he said, "and crush the truth a little in taking hold of it." The public reaction following the broadcast confirmed a long-developing skepticism concerning the public's ability to determine the truth of media reports. The Welles quotation is from Hadley Cantril with Hazel Gaudet and Herta Herzog, *The Invasion from Mars: A Study in the Psychology of Panic* (Princeton, NJ, 1940), p. 164. The stereotype, says Lippmann, in a phrase that speaks for one of his continuing intellectual preoccupations, is a pattern of thought that, unfortunately, preserves us "from all the bewildering effects of trying to see the world steadily and see it whole" (Walter Lippmann, *Public Opinion*, p. 114). See also chaps. 17 and 21–24, esp. pp. 363, 248–49, 170–71. One of several important corrective studies concerning the much-exaggerated accounts of the "hysteria" presumably caused by the Welles broadcast is found in Brad Schwartz, *Broadcast Hysteria: Orson Welles's War of the Worlds and the Art of Fake News* (New York, 2015).

pp. 110-114.

Leonard Doob, *Propaganda*, p. 151; V. O. Key, *Public Opinion and American Democracy* (New York, 1961), p. 357; George Sylvester Viereck, *Spreading Germs of Hate*, p. xvi; Walter Lippmann, *Public Opinion*, pp. 418, 395–97; Mark Sullivan, *Our Times*, vol. 5, p. 83; William Allen White, quoted in Reo N. Christenson and Robert Q. McWilliams, *Voice of the People: Readings in Public Opinion and Propaganda* (New York, 1962), p. 156; Walter Lippmann, *Public Opinion*, pp. 398–401, 411–14; Walter Lippmann, *Preface to Politics*, pp. 299ff.; Harold D. Lasswell, "Propaganda and Mass Insecurity," *Psychiatry* 13 (August 1950); Harold D. Lasswell, *Democracy Through Public Opinion* (Menasha, WI, 1941), p. 39; John Dewey, *The Public and Its Problems*, pp. 182–84; Thurman Arnold, *The Symbols of Government* (New York, 1935); Thurman Arnold, *The Folklore of Capitalism* (New Haven, CT, 1937), pp. 344, 205; Phillip Kennicott, "Where to Meet Real Americans, Touring Presidential Homes," *Washington Post*, October 16, 2016; also in the *Washington Post*, "Mount Rushmore Is Colossal Kitsch, Perfect for a Populist Spectacle," July 4, 2020.

pp. 114-117.

Dorothy Thompson, "Propaganda in the Modern World," *Vital Speeches* 2 (November 4, 1935); Ernest Hemingway, *A Farewell to Arms* (New York, 1929), chap. 27; Stuart Chase, *The Tyranny of Words* (New York, 1935), p. 171; C. K.

Ogden and I. A. Richards, *The Meaning of Meaning* (New York, 1925); Daniel J. Boorstin, *The Image, or What Happened to the American Dream* (New York, 1962); Walter Lippmann, *The Phantom Public*, pp. 38–44, 63, 70, 126ff., 189; Graham Wallas, *The Great Society*, p. 368; John Dewey, *The Public and Its Problems*, pp. 211–19; Walter Lippmann, *The Public Philosophy*, chap. 11; Walter Lippmann, *Public Opinion*, chap. 28, esp. p. 314. Lippmann eloquently echoed these same sentiments in his often-overlooked Lecture Series at the University of Virginia in 1927. See Walter Lippmann, *American Inquisitors* (New York, 2017), pp, 115-120.